Parenting by the Psalms

Sequel to *Parenting by the Parables*

Aubrey Johnson, Editor

Table of Contents

About this Book

Your child has a hero inside. It is your job to help them realize and utilize their God-given superpowers. Spiritual capacities like faith, hope, and love are powerful indeed. This book will show you how to unleash your child's potential and prepare them to meet life's demands.

Parenting by the Psalms was written for adults, but the focus is on the child, not the parent. For example, if a child is worried, how could a parent (or grandparent) use Psalm 23 to alleviate their child's anxiousness? The chapters are more pragmatic than didactic and more motivational than moralistic. The aim is to equip, not just exhort. Think of these chapters as abundant life tools (John 10.10).

Psalms are part of the Wisdom Literature of the Old Testament. What better book could parents turn to for wisdom to prepare their children to live faithfully and successfully? The more you ponder them, the more discerning and far-sighted you become. With poetic power, they guide, comfort, and spur you to live your best life.

So imagine what will happen when you introduce your children to this inspired collection of life-changing teachings. They will be less fearful and more confident and capable. The book of Psalms addresses most of the major issues people face during their lifetimes on earth. Do you wish someone had shared these insights with you at an early age? Why not do for your child what you wish someone had done for you (Matthew 7.12)?

Do not doubt that children can understand and apply the principles in the Psalms. This book will help you make those ideas reachable to young souls. Simple illustrations and practical applications allow you to achieve breakthroughs in spiritual understanding.

With assistance from 13 gifted communicators (ministers, counselors, and professors), you will be prepared to make the most of teachable moments with the confidence that can only come from Scripture. God's word is not a shot in the dark. It is a lamp to parents' feet and a light to your child's way. Give them God's light to lighten their load.

Parents prepare children to navigate the road ahead. The Psalms are pothole-filling gems of wisdom to overcome life's road hazards that lie in wait. Do not leave your kids defenseless. Help them practice the Psalms to live successfully and eternally.

Aubrey Johnson, Editor

Foreword

Roy Johnson

Executive Director L2L

There is nothing dearer to my heart than godly parenting. It is one of my primary reasons for working to further God's kingdom through Lads to Leaders (L2L). My wife, Brenda, and I raised three amazing, Christian young men. Perfect, no, but all three are first responders helping their communities. More importantly, they love the Lord and His church. Our primary goal was to raise men to love God, serve Christ, and bless others. We made mistakes, but our knees were often bowed in prayer for assistance as we raised them.

How I wish we had this valuable tool, *Parenting by the Psalms* by Aubrey Johnson, as a guide. Aubrey says it best: "If you start down the wrong road, you will end up in the wrong place" (Matthew 7.13-14). Parenting in today's social climate is peril-filled! What was once right is now considered wrong. The solution is to fill our hearts and homes with God's word. More than ever, parents need to feel the weight of their responsibility to "bring them up in the nurture and admonition of the Lord" (Ephesians 6.4).

The statistics are sobering. We have a new generation that, for the most part, does not know God and does not consider Him when making decisions. The answer is better parenting. Please use this valuable tool in raising your children, and pray every day for wisdom to guide them in the proper direction. Godly servants are not randomly made but are created with loving, wise hands following God's word for guidance. God gave you these beautiful souls to nurture in His love. Always seek Him in prayer!

"This book should be in every Christian parent's hands." —Roy Johnson

Chapter One

Psalm 1 - Be Like a Tree

Aubrey Johnson

Blessed is the man who walks not in the counsel of the wicked, nor stands in the way of sinners, nor sits in the seat of scoffers; but his delight is in the law of the LORD, and on his law he meditates day and night. He is like a tree planted by streams of water that yields its fruit in its season, and its leaf does not wither. In all that he does, he prospers. The wicked are not so, but are like chaff that the wind drives away. Therefore the wicked will not stand in the judgment, nor sinners in the congregation of the righteous; for the LORD knows the way of the righteous, but the way of the wicked will perish. (Psalm 1.1-6)

Help your child visualize this scene. Imagine you are sitting on a riverbank under a tree in the heat of the day. A cool wind rolls off of the water, refreshing your spirit. The shade beneath the tree's leafy branches delights you. Best of all, it is the season when ripe fruit hangs low. Brightly colored apples bounce gently in the wind, motioning you to come closer for a taste. Your mouth waters as you reach for a treat.

This charming scene envisions the life God wants for His people. You are the tree, healthy and strong, drinking freely from the stream of Scripture, and producing spiritual fruit in abundance. Your days on earth are pleasing and productive.

Just as the flowing river brings a bountiful harvest to farmers, the faithful enjoy fruitful lives by drinking in God's word.

Choose Your Environment

Children and trees flourish under the right conditions. In Psalm 1, the key to the tree's success is its ideal location. In another spot, its fortunes would be less certain. A tree planted by a river has a constant source of water. Consequently, it is less dependent on the weather. Rain is unpredictable. Rivers are more reliable. Trees cannot choose their setting, but God lets people have a say in their environment. So w*here* do you thrive spiritually? *How* will you invest your time? *With whom* will you spend your days? Healthy growth conditions can help you live successfully, and to find the best growth environment, ask yourself three questions:

- What is the *meaning* of success?
- What is the *source* of success?
- What is the *proof* of success?

What Is the Meaning of Success?

Like a healthy tree, a godly person prospers in all that he does (Psalm 1.3). To "prosper" is to *do well* and to *fare well*. Spiritual health is observable in worthy goals and godly growth. What are some ways your child wants to grow? What are some goals they hope to achieve? Make no mistake: God wants your child to succeed in life.

"Succeed" Is a Bible Word

- 2 Chronicles 20.20: "Believe in the Lord your God, and you will be established; believe his prophets and you will *succeed*."

- Proverbs 15.22: "Without counsel plans fail, but with many advisers they *succeed*."

To "succeed" is to produce a desired outcome. In spiritual terms, it is achieving God-pleasing ends. The secret to succeeding is to follow God's word and godly advice (1 Thessalonians 2.13). Faith prompts healthy behaviors that lead to big blessings. You "prosper" when faith-informed choices (1) honor God, (2) bless your neighbor, and (3) improve your character. Positive outcomes result from obedience to God.

Solomon wrote, "If the iron is blunt, and one does not sharpen the edge, he must use more strength, but wisdom helps one to *succeed*" (Ecclesiastes 10.10). Just as you sharpen an ax, you must sharpen your mind to cut through tough problems. Ask your child how people can improve their minds (and morals). Without a commitment to self-improvement, life is as difficult as cutting down a big tree with a dull blade (Matthew 13.15). However, mental and spiritual dullness are avoidable (Hebrews 5.11).

"Success" Is Experiencing a Favorable Outcome

The word "succeed" is a verb that emphasizes faithful action. The word "success" is a noun that stresses fruitful outcomes. Success is the result of succeeding in your undertakings. It is the harvest of good things that follows effective action.

- Joshua 1.7: "Only be strong and very courageous, being careful to do according to all the law that Moses my servant commanded you. Do not turn from it to the right hand or to the left, that you may have good *success* wherever you go."

- 1 Samuel 18.14: "And David had *success* in all his undertakings, for the LORD was with him."

Success in your endeavors comes from carefully following God's instructions. That makes the Bible the ultimate success manual. How your children look at the Bible makes a big difference in their future. The Bible is an exciting book because it equips you for life. God gives success to those who trust and obey Him. When His word directs you, He is surely with you.

When your life is (1) consistent with biblical precepts and (2) backed up by persistent prayers, you enjoy the best possible life. Therefore, if you want to be successful, do not forget to pray!

- Nehemiah 1.11: "O Lord, let your ear be attentive to the prayer of your servant, and to the prayer of your servants who delight to fear your name, and give *success* to your servant today, and grant him mercy in the sight of this man."

- Psalm 118.25: "Save us, we pray, O LORD! O LORD, we pray, give us *success*!"

Failing Is Falling Short

The opposite of prospering is failing. Unholy influences can hasten your fall (Psalm 1.1). When you hang out with people who are *immoral* (lacking principles), *intemperate* (lacking discipline), or *irreligious* (lacking faith), you are asking for trouble. Especially when they are *impenitent* (lacking remorse). Ask your child to explain the difference between a good friend and a bad friend. Discuss why people make poor choices about whom to befriend.

What Is the Source of Success?

Nearness to the river is the difference between a tree being barren or fruitful. Spiritually speaking, the proximity of the tree to the river represents the nearness of your heart to God's word. Do you delight in it and meditate on it? Do you frequent it day and night? God's word is to your soul what water is to a tree: a source of life. You cannot thrive without it. Successful people are drawn to God's word. They want more of it rather than less. They know it makes their lives better. Ask your children what they love about God's word.

In a secondary sense, think of the river as the flow of faith-filled people you encounter during your lifetime. Paul said, "Faith comes by hearing, and hearing by the word of God" (Romans 10.17). According to Jesus, when the word of God dwells in someone, their influence is a steady stream of blessings to all they encounter (John 7.37-39).

> On the last day of the feast, the great day, Jesus stood up and cried out, "If anyone thirsts, let him come to me and drink. Whoever believes in me, as the Scripture has said, 'Out of his heart will flow rivers of living water.'" Now this he said about the Spirit, whom those who believed in him were to receive, for as yet the Spirit had not been given, because Jesus was not yet glorified.

By living and sharing Jesus' teachings, godly people become a source of your success. Then when you model and share Jesus' words, you become a source of spiritual success to others. "The fruit of the righteous is a tree of life, and whoever captures souls is wise" (Proverbs 11.30).

People come and go throughout your lifetime, but their influence lingers. For example, godly parents raise children in the discipline and instruction of the Lord (Ephesians 6.4), and good friends strengthen good morals (1 Corinthians 15.33). Encourage your children to be a positive force in the lives of others but also to choose people of faith as their closest friends. Spiritually healthy people strengthen your character and enrich your life. Unsafe people defile your character and diminish your life.

God sends people into your life to bless and improve you. Satan sends people into your life to confuse and corrupt you. God sends and Satan sends, but you choose. Godly friends are spiritual tributaries that feed your success. Choose good friends who encourage you. Choose faithful brethren who exhort you. Choose wise teachers who enlighten you. Choose sound preachers who edify you. Ask your children to name some people who help them get better. What do these people do that is helpful?

What Is the Fruit of Success?

Usefulness is a sign of fruitfulness, and wise planting is crucial for bearing good fruit. Choosing your associates is a form of planting. When you make a friend, you put down relational roots to feed your soul. Jonathan chose David, Elisha chose Elijah, Timothy chose Paul, Peter chose John, and Priscilla chose Aquila. Few choices matter more than whom to befriend. Most of all, follow Abraham's example and choose to be friends with God (James 2.23). Abraham epitomizes what it means to be successful. His life was fruitful because he was faithful.

Faithful people are active and effective. Their faith is proven genuine by what they do (James 2.17). Their words and works correspond with God's word. By aligning themselves with God's will, they prove they are friends of God rather than friends of the world (James 4.4).

Jesus said, "You are my friends if you do what I command you" (John 15.14). There is a clear link between genuine friendship, obedient faith, and fruitful living. Just as a fertile tree produces bountiful fruit, so a faithful heart produces a beneficial life (Matthew 7.18). "You will recognize them by their fruits" (Matthew 7.16).

High character, healthy relationships, and holy accomplishments are examples of God-honoring fruit: "for the fruit of light is found in all that is good and right and true" (Ephesians 5.9). Where there is no goodness there is no godliness (Galatians 5.22-23), and where there is no fruit there is no faith (James 2.26). Foolish people are useless because their faith is inactive, incomplete, and thus inconsequential (James 2.20-22). Wise people are commendable because their faith is profitable (Matthew 25.21).

Good Choices, Good Fruit

In Psalm 1, the man of God is blessed because of good choices. His love for God's word and godly friends eliminated bad choices. He knew—in advance—where he would not sit, stand, or walk. Consequently, he never started down the wrong road. The choice to live for God simplifies and beautifies your life.

Small compromises lead to bigger ones (James 1.14-15). Choosing a friend sets in motion a series of events, and selecting ungodly companions leads to foreseeable and regrettable outcomes. Ask your child what the future holds when you become close friends with someone who has no desire to please God.

Better Friends, Better Future

Using three examples, the psalmist warns readers not to befriend those who boldly defy God's will:

- **The wicked** - Unfeeling people who harm others to fulfill their desires.
  Do not walk in their counsel.
- **Sinners** - Evil doers who brazenly violate the protective boundaries of God's word.
  Do not stand in their way.

- **Scoffers** - Shameless cynics who deny the benefits of living God's way.

  Do not sit in their seat.

If you start down the wrong road, you will end up in the wrong place (Matthew 7.13-14). A (1) wicked act leads to a (2) sinful life that is reinforced by a (3) cynical attitude. One thing follows the other like night follows day. When you choose your friends you are choosing your future. Are they holy or hardened; righteous or remorseless; pious or pernicious? God lets you choose, and successful people make better choices than unsuccessful people.

Success Is Not Accidental

When you plant your soul by rivers of living water, success is far more likely. Encourage your child to spend more time with God's word and with godly people who will encourage them to pursue wisdom and holiness. Sadly, most people do not consciously choose their future. They are not successful because they are not intentional.

Teach your children not to accept randomness in life. Teach them the foundational principles of success from Psalm 1. First, choose what you want (be purposeful and precise). Second, create conditions for growth (build good habits and good friendships). Third, cast seeds of success (behave faithfully and consistently). The day of harvest will not disappoint those who follow these simple but powerful steps.

This chapter began with three questions and now ends with three solid answers confirmed by God's word. (1) The meaning of success is *faithfulness*, (2) the source of success is *fellowship*, and (3) the proof of success is *fruitfulness*. God wants every child to succeed, and parents are an important part of His plan. May God bless you as you share the psalmist's secrets of success.

Practicing the Psalms

To be successful, choose good friends.

Text Questions:
1. What was the tree planted beside?
2. What did the tree yield in its season?
3. What are the wicked like?
4. In what do blessed people delight?
5. When do they delight in it?

Discussion Questions:
1. How are people like trees? How are they different?
2. What do trees need to grow well?
3. What do people need to grow well?
4. What happens when trees are water-deprived?
5. What happens when people are word-deprived?

Parent/Child Exercise: Visit a nearby river or creek lined with trees. Start a discussion with your children about trees and the benefits of growing near a steady water supply. Next, read Psalm 1 together. Use the questions above to guide your conversation. Point out that people, unlike trees, can choose their growth environment. Most people who fall in with the wrong crowd do not go down the wrong path on purpose. They simply fail to make a better choice. Ask your children what kind of friends they will choose. Ask them what kind of habits they will build. Have them tell you why daily Bible study is essential for a fruitful life.

Chapter Two

Psalm 19 - Listen to the Stars

Ryan N. Fraser

The heavens declare the glory of God, and the sky above proclaims his handiwork. Day to day pours out speech, and night to night reveals knowledge. There is no speech, nor are there words, whose voice is not heard. Their voice goes out through all the earth, and their words to the end of the world. In them he has set a tent for the sun, which comes out like a bridegroom leaving his chamber, and, like a strong man, runs its course with joy. Its rising is from the end of the heavens, and its circuit to the end of them, and there is nothing hidden from its heat. (Psalm 19.1-6)

Sunrises and sunsets are extraordinary things. Have you ever taken the time to watch a sunrise or sunset with your children? It is especially inspiring to behold these displays of God's artistry by the ocean. I grew up in South Africa near the coast. Standing with my parents and siblings on the beach at sunset while singing, "Have You Seen Jesus, My Lord," left an indelible impression on my soul. The gradually changing color palette of God's immense canvas was breathtaking. Radiant sunrays beamed through the clouds. Shimmering reflections of light nimbly danced across the waves. God's calming presence was palpable. Be purposeful in planning for your children to experience such marvels firsthand—to see God's masterful paintbrush decorate the sky with brilliant colors: yellows, oranges, reds, pinks, and violets–to be still and know that He is God (Psalm 46.10).

Experience God's Handiwork Together

When a family watches a sunrise or sunset together it bonds them. Shared experiences do that. It also opens the heart and mind to God's presence and His preservation of the universe: everything and everyone in it. The formation of faith is largely experiential by nature. These special experiences open the door for unforced conversations about God's greatness and goodness. Romans 1.19-20 asserts, "For what can be known about God is plain to them, because God has shown it to them. For his invisible attributes, namely, his eternal power and divine nature, have been clearly perceived, ever since the creation of the world, in the things that have been made. So they are without excuse."

Taking your children to an unlit area outside of town on a clear night provides another opportunity to experience the wonder of the cosmos as stars sparkle in the firmament. Who knows, you might even see a shooting star or satellite cross the sky. The constancy of the constellations displays divine order, and their precise placement evidence a mysterious but masterful design. Visiting planetariums and observatories are stirring experiences for young and old alike. Who can forget their first view of the heavens through a high-powered telescope? Contemplating the cosmos is a soulful experience as much as a scientific one.

The psalmist exclaims, "The heavens declare the glory of God, and the sky above proclaims his handiwork. Day to day pours out speech, and night to night reveals knowledge" (Psalm 19.1-2). The stars and planets transmit a persuasive message about their Creator. The immensity, grandeur, and splendor of the Milky Way are awe-inspiring. Astronomers estimate there are between 100 and 400 billion stars in the Milky Way alone. But only in the past few decades have we come to realize that the Milky Way is only one of 100 billion galaxies in the universe and that its disk stretches some 100,000 light-years across.

Become an Amateur Astronomer

Educate yourself on the location of the five bright planets in their outward order from the sun: Mercury, Venus, Mars, Jupiter, and Saturn (you can see these with the naked eye). Be ready to identify them when looking upward to the heavens. Some phenomenal, free cell phone apps will greatly assist you in this endeavor. Then take the time to point the planets and astral systems out to your children. Remind them that God created these magnificent celestial bodies. These are the same planets and stars watched by our ancestors over the millennia. By the way, did you know that the easiest way to pick out planets is to remember this basic rule of thumb: stars twinkle, and planets don't? Become familiar with the major constellations so you can identify them in the night sky for your wide-eyed children. It will be a door opener for deeper conversations with your children regarding the eternal existence and unlimited power of God.

Take Your Kids Back to the Beginning

Teach your children that, "In the beginning, God created the heavens and the earth" (Genesis 1.1). Emphasize this foundational biblical truth! Then read together Genesis 1.14-18 to learn more about the creation process. Every detail reveals more about God's wisdom, love, and power. Ask your children what they think about these verses and if they have any questions about their significance. This could be yet another great conversation starter! You may want to ask your children to draw or paint a picture that illustrates this inspired passage that you could display prominently in your home. By drawing or painting an image, they will process the meaning and importance at a deeper level.

The Transmission of Faith

Moving from tangibles (the material) to intangibles (the spiritual) can be a bit tricky when it comes to faith development and spiritual formation in your children. However, it is not impossible. It just requires some intentionality and time. The process of faith transmission between parent and child follows a gradual, well-paced pattern. Solid faith development will move from what is seen to what is unseen or from the visible to the invisible. Therefore, it will gradually transition from the concrete to the more abstract.

Biblical faith is not blind at all. Neither is it a leap into the dark. Rather, it is an intelligent faith founded on sound reason and factual content that is based on convincing evidence. The magnificent galaxies and beautifully designed constellations all point directly to God. They speak volumes about their almighty, eternal Creator!

Stages of Faith Development

In his book *Will Our Children Have Faith?* (New York: Seabury Press, 1976), John H. Westerhoff III suggests that faith grows like the rings of a tree. Each ring adds to and changes the tree by building on that which has grown before. With this vivid metaphor in mind, he proposes four rings in the faith development process:

Ring #1: Experienced Faith (2 Timothy 1.5)

At the core is the faith which we experience from our earliest and most impressionable years in childhood. We essentially inherit the faith of our primary caregivers and guardians, likely our parents and grandparents. The way our parents' faith shapes their lives makes an indelible impression on us, creating the core (first ring) of our faith.

Ring #2: Affiliative Faith (Romans 12.2)

Another ring is formed as preteens and young adolescents gradually internalize the beliefs, values, and practices of their family, group, or church. Teenagers take on the characteristics of nurturing persons and become identified as members of the faith tradition. This identification may be formalized through baptism and placing membership with a congregation. This phase of a young person's development is recognized as a time of testing and attempting to gain group (and peer) acceptance. Children develop a sense of personal belonging, religious identity, and conformity in belief and practice.

Ring #3: Searching Faith (1 Thessalonians 5.21)

Faith development reaches a crucial junction when a child becomes aware that his or her personal beliefs may no longer be identical to those of the group. He or she may begin to question some of the commonly held beliefs or practices of their faith tradition. As time goes on, a decision must be reached: "Do I take responsibility for my religious beliefs or merely accept my group's norms regarding faith and practice?"

Ring #4: Owned Faith (Philippians 2.12-13)

The faith development process culminates in the expression of a personally-owned and acknowledged faith. The individual reorients his or her life and now claims responsibility for adhered-to beliefs and practices.

An Entry Point into the Word of God

For our present chapter, our interest focuses on Rings 1 and 2 above. The important role of parents in their children's faith development cannot be overemphasized. A parent's spiritual teaching, influence, and religious example are essential. As Deuteronomy 6.4-9 bears out in the Shema, the concept of faith in God must be woven throughout the fabric of daily family life so that it becomes a natural, seamless conversation from rising in the morning to lying down at bedtime. Talking about God as Creator and Sustainer of the universe is one way to enter into this conversation spontaneously.

As the earth rotates, the predictable circuit of the sun from dawn to dusk gives a sense of constancy and design to God's magnificent creation. The warmth of the sun cheers hearts and facilitates life (Psalm 19.6). These natural laws are a reflection of God's spiritual laws found in His perfect and holy Word. Natural laws bring order to the outer world, and spiritual laws bring order to the inner world.

The law of the LORD is perfect, reviving the soul; the testimony of the LORD is sure, making wise the simple; the precepts of the LORD are right, rejoicing the heart; the commandment of the LORD is pure, enlightening the eyes; the fear of the LORD is clean, enduring forever; the rules of the LORD are true, and righteous altogether. (Psalm 19.7-9)

Notice that God's Word is referred to in various ways in this text. Each description serves as a lens through which to perceive God's inspired revelation.

1. The *law* of the LORD is perfect, reviving the soul.
2. The *testimony* of the LORD is sure, making wise the simple.
3. The *precepts* of the LORD are right, rejoicing the heart.
4. The *commandment* of the LORD is pure, enlightening the eyes.
5. The *fear* of the LORD is clean, enduring forever.
6. The *rules* of the LORD are true and righteous altogether.

God's Word is characterized by seven superlatives. Its perfection, surety, rightness, purity, cleanness, trueness, and righteousness are the fulfillment of the magnificent and glorious cosmic order. Remember how the magi, or wise men, followed the new star in the sky to find baby Jesus, the promised messiah (Matthew 2.1-2). Jesus Christ himself is identified as the Word (John 1.1), Creator (John 1.3), Life (John 1.4), and Light (John 1.4-5). His teachings and example bring order to our lives.

The Value of God's Word

In Psalm 19.10-11, David contends that the Word of God is "More to be desired . . . than gold, even much fine gold; sweeter also than honey and drippings of the honeycomb. Moreover, by them is your servant warned; in keeping them there is great reward." The Bible's value is inestimable, and its sweetness is incomparable. It provides a clear guide for pleasing the Lord to be eternally rewarded by Him. The perfect will of God keeps our feet from straying off the path of righteousness and falling into sin's trap (Psalm 19.12-13).

The ultimate goal of the psalmist is given as follows: "Let the words of my mouth and the meditation of my heart be acceptable in your sight, O LORD, my rock and my redeemer" (Psalm 19.14). He wants his faith in God to be (1) solidly placed and (2) properly manifested. And that is what we should also desire for our precious children: to learn and live the will of our Creator who designed us to shine like stars.

Practicing the Psalms

To be successful, shine like stars.

26

Text Questions:
1. What do the heavens declare about God?
2. What humanlike thing are the heavens doing?
3. What rises from the ends of the heavens and moves to the end of them?
4. What is perfect and revives the soul?
5. The Word of God is to be more desired than what?

Discussion Questions:
1. How is God's Word like the heavens (solar system)?
2. When we witness sunrises, what can we tell about God?
3. Why did God create the planets and stars?
4. What is your favorite star constellation and why?
5. What makes God's Word so very valuable to us?

Parent/Child Exercise: Download a free stargazing app (such as "Star Chart") to your cell phone. Then, on a clear night, take a family excursion to a quiet location on the outskirts of town, beyond the city lights. Work together as a family to identify various planets and star constellations. Next, read Psalm 19 together. Use the questions above to guide your conversation. Point out that God uses His majestically created universe to reveal some very important things to us about His nature. God's Word also tells us a lot about who God is and about His perfect will for our lives. Why is the Bible more precious than gold and sweeter than honey?

Chapter Three
Psalm 23 - Know Your Shepherd
James Dalton

The Lord is my shepherd; I shall not want. He makes me lie down in green pastures. He leads me beside still waters. He restores my soul. He leads me in paths of righteousness for his name's sake. Even though I walk through the valley of the shadow of death, I will fear no evil, for you are with me; your rod and your staff, they comfort me. You prepare a table before me in the presence of my enemies; you anoint my head with oil; my cup overflows. Surely goodness and mercy shall follow me all the days of my life, and I shall dwell in the house of the LORD forever. (Psalm 23.1-6)

Many well-meaning and studious people of faith have taught that worry is sinful. After all, Jesus said, "Do not be worried" (Matthew 6.25, NASB) and Paul taught "do not be anxious about anything" (Philippians 4.6). However, the Bible records the worries of many righteous people. Paul worried about shipwreck and death (Acts 27.10). Abraham worried he would be killed for his wife (Genesis 12 and 20). Gideon worried his army would be defeated (Judges 7.7-11). Jesus worried His apostles might forsake Him (John 6.66-71). On the night of His betrayal, He worried about the coming events. Luke described His mental pain as "agony" (Luke 22.44). The Greek word for "agony" can also mean "apprehensive" or "distressed."

Worrying itself is not sinful and pressuring a child to never worry is typically counterproductive. However, worrying can become sinful in some situations:

- Worrying so much about physical things that you are distracted from spiritual things (Matthew 6.19-24).
- Failing to bring worries to God in prayer and trying to handle them all on your own (1 Peter 5.6 7).
- Growing contented with overwhelming worry instead of seeking a healthier perspective (Matthew 25.25).

While worrying is not always sinful, it is not where God wants us to stay. Instead, God wants to share our concerns. When our child is worried—about how they will do on their presentation tomorrow; that they will not fit in at their new school; that the coach might not pick them to start the game; or that they might not make the honor roll—we know that the problem will be short-lived in comparison to the length of their life.

However, as a father who truly loves my child, I try to feel and demonstrate concern because they are concerned (Romans 12.15). I want them to know when they have problems, worries, or fears that I will be there to help them through these things. My heavenly Father is perfect. Even though He knows my worries are short-lived in the scheme of eternity, He cares because they are currently bothering me, and He wants to share that burden with me. That is why He tells me to cast my anxieties on Him in prayer (1 Peter 5.7).

God wants better for me than worry. He wants me to be able to reduce worrying by healthier thinking and living. This is the message about worrying that we should be teaching our children today. Teach your child that Jesus worried, that Gideon worried, that Paul worried. But also teach them that God wants us to learn how to worry less so we can have more healthy and productive lives.

Develop Healthy Thoughts

Christians are urged to think about good things (Philippians 4.8). Psalm 23 contains examples of healthy thinking. When a person with anxiety or worry focuses on these types of healthy thoughts, it helps them to overcome the unhealthy thoughts of excessive worry. The healthy messages communicated in Psalm 23 can be taught to children to help them develop healthy thoughts.

"The Lord is my shepherd" (Psalm 23.1).

While God is the shepherd of many, His relationship with me is personal, unique, and special. God is willing to leave the flock in the wilderness and seek me out when I am lost (Matthew 18.12-14). Children should be taught that God cares about them individually. He formed them in the womb (Jeremiah 1.5) and knows how many hairs they have on their head (Luke 12.7). Your child should remember that God knows them, loves them, and wants a relationship with them.

"I shall not want. He makes me lie down in green pastures; He leads me beside still waters" (Psalm 23.1-2).

God provides good things for His sheep. He gives the necessities of life (Matthew 6.33) and helps His sheep be content where needs are lacking (Philippians 4.11-13). Children should be taught that God will provide for them. He will not give them all they desire, but when they follow Him, He will ensure they have what they need (2 Corinthians 9.8).

"He restores my soul. He leads me in paths of righteousness for His name's sake" (Psalm 23.3).

God replenishes me and helps me live in a way that brings glory to Him. Children often worry about messing up or not pleasing their friends and family. While every one of us will make mistakes, God is willing to forgive and restore us. Children should be taught that God will help them do right and help them be restored when they fail (1 Corinthians 10.13; 1 John 1.7-2.2).

"Even though I walk through the valley of the shadow of death, I will fear no evil, for You are with me; Your rod and Your staff, they comfort me" (Psalm 23.4).

Every person will go through some dark days and painful valleys. Children should be taught that in times of suffering, God has promised, "I will never leave you nor forsake you" (Hebrews 13.5; Deuteronomy 31.6; Joshua 1.5; 1 Chronicles 28.20).

"You prepare a table before me in the presence of my enemies" (Psalm 23.5).

Even when enemies are present, God's sheep do not have to fear them, because He is here, and He is more powerful than those enemies could ever hope to be. Children should be taught to turn toward God when enemies distract them with hateful words or hurtful deeds. They should be taught to remember that God is stronger than their enemies.

"My cup overflows" (Psalm 23.5).

The blessings from God truly cannot be numbered (James 1.17). When we are worried about what might happen or current problems, we often overlook these innumerable blessings. Children should be taught to notice the overwhelming number of blessings from God, even when something unpleasant occurs.

"Surely goodness and mercy shall follow me all the days of my life" (Psalm 23.6).

Good and mercy exist and can be found even during the most severe persecutions that have occurred. Children should be taught that when we are worried about the negatives that may happen, we should also remind ourselves that goodness and mercy will exist no matter how bad things may become.

"And I shall dwell in the house of the Lord forever" (Psalm 23.6).

The ultimate goal of every person should be to live eternally in Heaven with God the Father. Those who "walk in the light," confessing and repenting of their stumbles, can be confident of forgiveness and salvation (1 John 1.7-10; 2.28; 5.13). Children should be taught that following God and eternally living with Him is what matters in life, and that salvation is not in question when they follow Him.

Imagine the change that can occur when a worrisome person moves their thinking away from the negative things that might occur and toward the positive things we know with confidence. Children may worry, "What if I fail that test?" "What if my friend does not like me anymore?" "What if I do not make the team?" "What if I forget to do my homework?" The list of "what ifs" is limitless. Instead, help your child focus on the many certainties we can know:

- God wants a personal relationship with me.
- God will provide for me.
- God will help me do right and forgive me when I fail.
- God will not leave me.
- God will help me be better.
- God is bigger than my problems and enemies.
- God's blessings are innumerable.
- God's goodness and mercy can always be found.
- God wants me to be with Him for all eternity.

The process of changing how one thinks is possible. Counseling can help with situations where a child experiences debilitating anxiety. To begin at home, however, help your child try this approach. Every time they are worried, help them remind themselves of three of these thoughts from Psalm 23. When the mind wanders back to worrying, again they should remind themselves of these helpful and healthy thoughts. Repeatedly doing this will establish more healthy thinking patterns.

Take Healthy Actions

In addition to developing more healthy *thinking*, worrying can be addressed by *doing* more healthy things.

"He leads me beside still waters" (Psalm 23.2).

Remember that calm waters are mentioned in David's list of what God provides. Life can become very busy and hectic with schedules so overfull that we jump from one event to the next. When schedules are overfull, they are typically filled with unnecessary desires that leave little room for spiritual activities. One thing you can control is to seek the calmness that God wants for His sheep. Limit the number of distractions and events in your life so that you have time to slow down and spend quality time with your children. When time is reclaimed, use it to help them grow in their connection to God.

"He restores my soul. He leads me in paths of righteousness for His name's sake" (Psalm 23.3).

Our children should be taught to be attentive to the choices they make—but be careful. Some children become so overwhelmed with the responsibility to do right that they miss the nature of God's grace and become anxious about the impossibility of perfection. This leaves them feeling frustrated and hopeless. However, more individuals allow physical distractions to become their focus (Matthew 13.22). God tells us that we can only have one master (Matthew 6.24), so help your children learn to focus on making Him the Master of their lives while trusting His grace to cover their many imperfections.

Invest in a Healthy Attitude

Beyond implementing more healthy thinking and more healthy practices, worry can be addressed by developing more healthy attitudes.

Live in Today

While David recognized the good in the future (Psalm 23.6), his focus was primarily on the present day. Worry and anxiety are closely associated with fear, but there is an important difference. Fear is experienced when someone believes there is a threat in the immediate moment (a vicious dog running at them or being startled by a loud noise). Worry and anxiety, on the other hand, are experienced when one is thinking about what might happen in the future. When we are overly worried about the future, we need to shift our focus to the here and now – what is going on in the moment (Matthew 6.34; James 4.13-17). Children should be encouraged to experience today without feeling pressure about the future. Tomorrow is not here yet, and it will never be exactly what we imagine it to be!

Trust in God

David's overall theme in Psalm 23 is trust in and reliance on God. An abundance of things affect you and are beyond your control. You could easily worry about the effects that world events, illnesses, or other calamities can have upon your life. Instead of worrying about what you cannot control, a healthier attitude to develop is one of trust. This is not a blind optimism that things will always be good, but a calm assurance that no matter what happens, God can accomplish good (Romans 8.28). This trust involves confidence that God hears His children's concerns and wants good for them. This attitude of trust provides "the peace of God, which surpasses all understanding" (Philippians 4.6-7).

Conclusion

We try as parents (1) to repeat the patterns our parents instilled that worked well and (2) to avoid their mistakes. We hope and pray that, in the end, our children will be faithful and successful. There is no perfect parenting formula. No approach works the same with all children. That being said, the principles of Psalm 23 can be very effective in helping your child with worry. Help them develop healthy thinking, help them take healthy actions, and in so doing you will help them build healthy attitudes of trust and a focus on today.

Practicing the Psalms

To be successful, think healthy thoughts.

Text Questions:
1. To what is God comparable?
2. What kind of waters does He lead you beside?
3. What will God prepare in the presence of your enemies?
4. What will follow you all the days of your life?
5. Where can you dwell forever?

Discussion Questions:
1. Is worrying always wrong? When is worrying wrong?
2. What are your favorite thoughts from Psalm 23?
3. Does God promise to give us things we want or need?
4. Why focus on today instead of tomorrow?
5. What does it mean to trust God?

Parent/Child Exercise: Peaceful Breathing

The following technique is designed to be utilized when your child is struggling with worry. However, you should teach them this technique on days when worry is not a problem so that your child will be comfortable with what to do when it is needed.

Ask your child to sit in a comfortable chair and close their eyes. Ask them to quietly breathe in their nose, deeply and slowly, and then to let that air slowly out their mouth. Help them slow their breathing to where it takes about three seconds to breathe in and three seconds to breathe out. It may help to count 1-2-3 slowly with each breath in and out for a few cycles. After they have taken several breaths at this pace, tell them to continue this breathing while imagining a calm stream surrounded by green pastures with many sheep grazing peacefully. Give them about a minute to focus on this scene, while continuing the slow breathing. Then tell them to keep breathing the same way as they think the words, "The Lord is my shepherd" while breathing in, and to focus on the words, "I shall not want" while breathing out. Help them by saying these words as they breathe in and out for several cycles, getting quieter with each cycle until you are at a whisper and then again silent. Allow this slow breathing cycle to continue for another minute while they focus on the words of Psalm 23.1. Then tell your child that when they feel calm and at peace, they can open their eyes.

Progressive muscle relaxation, breathing exercises, meditation, and mindfulness are all techniques counselors teach people today to help with anxiety. The technique in the preceding paragraph draws several of these approaches together. If you or your child struggles excessively with anxiety, speaking to a counselor or another mental health professional is recommended.

References
Danker, F. W. (Ed.). (2000). *A Greek-English Lexicon of the New Testament and Other Early Christian Literature* (3rd ed., [BDAG]). The University of Chicago Press.

Chapter Four

Psalm 25 - Be Teachable

Aubrey Johnson

Good and upright is the LORD; therefore he instructs sinners in the way. He leads the humble in what is right, and teaches the humble his way. All the paths of the LORD are steadfast love and faithfulness, for those who keep his covenant and his testimonies. (Psalm 25.8-10)

Most parents want their children to be confident, but few parents are equally concerned with helping them to be humble. If forced to choose between the two, which would you want for your child? For me, it would be the latter—hands down. No such choice is necessary, but the value of humility is often overlooked. Every good thing you want for your child begins with this misunderstood, under-appreciated trait.

Humility is a modest view of your importance, especially in comparison with others. It is not thinking you are worthless, but rather it is understanding the equal value of people around you. Like you, they were made in God's image, and because of their intrinsic worth, you refuse to judge them based on worldly standards (houses, cars, clothes, degrees, positions). They are precious to God, so they are precious to you.

Humility is also a modest view of your knowledge, especially in comparison with God. It is staggering how little one person can know about the world's information on a single subject. Humility increases your capacity for learning because a teachable spirit is the foundation of wisdom. The more you think you know, the more ignorant you become. The more you realize how much you have to learn, the wiser you become. Humble people eagerly pursue God's wisdom (Matthew 5.6).

Blessed Are the Poor in Spirit

When Jesus preached the greatest sermon ever, He began with the all-time greatest list for self-improvement. The beatitudes include eight traits that Jesus guaranteed would turn an ordinary life into a blessed one (Matthew 5.3-12). Are you surprised to discover that the first thing on Jesus' list for living well and delighting God is humility? Jesus said, "Blessed are the poor in spirit." To be poor in something can be positive or negative depending on the quality being measured. To be lacking in love is bad, but to empty yourself of egotism is a blessing.

Poverty of "spirit" is a blessing because arrogance interferes with learning, growth, and service. A person swollen with pride is so full of himself that there is little room left for God's guidance or assistance. An inflated ego is a huge problem.

Theirs Is the Kingdom of Heaven

Jesus made an astounding promise to those who practice humility: "Blessed are the poor in spirit, for theirs is the kingdom of heaven." Only the humble can enter heaven or enjoy the beneficial teachings of the heavenly kingdom. No humility, no reservation or transformation. Why? Because the aspirations and deliberations of the proud are solely self-centered. When Cain killed Abel, he was thinking of himself, not his brother or his God. The selfish and sullen reject God's reign and have no place in His realm.

Humble people balance personal initiative with reliance on divine power. They work toward meaningful goals but give God the glory. Because of their dependence on God, they can endure disappointments without giving up (Philippians 4.12). The conceited are less capable of navigating life's ups and downs because they obsess about their persona and view life as a contest. Concerned with their image and interests, they find it difficult to celebrate others' successes or empathize with others' sorrows (Philippians 2.3-4).

Jesus said unless you become like little children, you cannot enter the "kingdom of heaven" (Matthew 18.3). Notice the similar wording between this statement and the first beatitude? Young children are known for humility. They are more open to instruction, correction, and guidance than many adults. Sadly, this trait can dwindle as people age. Staying humble is a lifetime challenge.

42

The Mystery of Humility

Jesus' birth affirmed the dignity of modesty, and His lifestyle modeled the beauty of simplicity, but His humble spirit was never more impressive than at Calvary. On the cross, the greatest man who ever lived submitted Himself to the will of God to save mankind. Because He lowered himself, God exalted Him. Remembering Jesus' example, James urges Christians to "Humble yourselves before the Lord, and He will exalt you" (James 4.10). James knew that humility is counterintuitive. Rather than diminishing you, it elevates you. The way up is down.

How do you teach your child to value humility and follow Christ's example? Psalm 25 is a perfect text for this purpose. The psalmist begins by praising God's admirable qualities and abundant provisions. He is good, upright, faithful, merciful, and loving. If your child is older, have them read the Psalm aloud to you while pausing to write down what it says about God. Ask how these traits make it a joy to humble yourself to the Lord.

Four Petitions of the Humble

Knowing God's goodness, the psalmist makes four requests:

1. **Lead Me** - "Lead me in your truth and teach me, for you are the God of my salvation." (Psalm 25.5)

God is ready to teach when you are ready to learn. Verse 9 says, "He leads the humble in what is right, and teaches the humble his way." Humility is the key to readiness. When children are ready to listen, God uses parents and teachers to guide them in His way. "Good and upright is the LORD; therefore he instructs sinners in the way" (Psalm 25.8). "The way" of the Bible is the best way to live. Because God's teachings bless and improve you, He is glorified whenever you obey Him (Matthew 5.16). "All the paths of the LORD are steadfast love and faithfulness, for those who keep his covenant and his testimonies. Lead me in your truth" (Psalm 25.10).

2. **Remember Me** - "Remember not the sins of my youth or my transgressions; according to your steadfast love, remember me, for the sake of your goodness, O Lord!" (Psalm 25.7)

God has a good memory. Not just good recall, but recall of what is good. No one wants to be remembered for their worst moment. The psalmist asks God to focus on the positive in his life instead of dwelling on the negative. Looking past others' shortcomings is a godly quality. You have lots of memories, but you choose what to spotlight. The writer pleads, "Remember your mercy, O LORD, and your steadfast love, for they have been from of old" (Psalm

25.6). God has a track record of kindness, so when you sin, do not turn away from God. You need Him more than ever. He knows your past, but He also knows your potential. If you are sorry for your sins and seeking to improve, He is merciful and faithful. Do not think you can hide your shortcomings from God. If you are sincere about spiritual growth and service, invite Him to inspect your heart. God knows your past but He also knows your penitence and progress.

3. **Deliver Me** - "Oh, guard my soul, and deliver me." (Psalm 25.20)

The psalmist was feeling down. He pleaded, "Turn to me and be gracious to me, for I am lonely and afflicted" (Psalm 25.16). He added, "The troubles of my heart are enlarged; bring me out of my distresses" (Psalm 25.17). Distresses are extreme sorrows, difficulties, and pains. Ask God to protect you from temptations and trials, but don't stop there (Matthew 613). Avoiding trouble is the best course, yet all of us get in over our heads at some point. When that happens, modify your prayer. Go from "guard me" to "deliver me." Don't get into trouble if you can help it, but if you do, look to the One who can help you get out of your jam. He helped Joseph in prison, David in disgrace, Daniel in a lion's den, and Jonah in a great fish. Whatever your problem, God is bigger.

4. **Forgive Me** - "Consider my affliction and my trouble, and forgive all my sins." (Psalm 25.18)

Ask for God's help, but also ask for His forgiveness. The psalmist asks God to remember how much he has already suffered. Sometimes suffering is due to sinful choices. When that is the case, the way forward begins with repentance and confession. Admit the source of your pain, and stop doing what is hurting you. The writer knows he does not deserve forgiveness, but he also knows that God loves to forgive those who sincerely seek His pardon. The writer adds, "May integrity and uprightness preserve me" (Psalm 25.21). Pursuing "integrity" and "uprightness" proves the genuineness of your repentance and gratitude for God's grace. You can't be perfect, but your life should show you are serious about living for God. Heartfelt obedience pleases your Father and preserves your soul.

Four Pledges of the Humble

In addition to making four petitions, the psalmist makes four promises to God. The psalmist says "I lift," "I trust," "I wait," and "I take refuge." God's continued blessings are conditioned on continued faithfulness. Let's take a closer look at these four pledges that can serve as a guide for our children.

1. **I Lift** - "To You O Lord, I lift up my soul." (Psalm 25.1)

A little later, the psalmist said, "My eyes are *ever* toward the Lord" (Psalm 25.15). Constantly looking to the Lord is the key to success (Hebrews 12.1-2). Paul urged the Christians in Colossae, "If then you have been raised with Christ, seek the things that are above, where Christ is, seated at the right hand of God. Set your minds on things that are above, not on things that are on earth" (Colossians 3.2). When you need answers, Scripture will lift up your soul. When you need assistance, prayer will lift up your soul. God uplifts those who lift up their soul to Him. The psalmist declared, "I lift up my eyes to the hills. From where does my help come? My help comes from the LORD, who made heaven and earth" (Psalm 121.1-2). When you lift up your soul to God—through worship, study, meditation, and prayer—He will lift you up.

2. **I Trust** - "O my God, in you I trust." (Psalm 25.2)

There is zero chance that God will let you down when you trust and obey Him. He may not do exactly what you want, but He will always do what is best (Romans 8.28). You are not smarter or stronger than God, so keep trusting even when you don't understand His ways or timing. When things seem harder or slower than you think they need to be, remember two things: God has a purpose in mind and a blessing in store (Proverbs 3.5-8). Obedience is a sign of trust. Disobedience shows that trust has dwindled.

3. **I Wait** - "For You, I wait all the day long." (Psalm 25.5)

When you are young, waiting is hard to do, but it is really important. Waiting well is a sign of humility and maturity. Unfortunately, some people never grow up. King Saul had trouble waiting (1 Samuel 13.8-14). He ruled a kingdom, but he could not rule himself. When he grew impatient, he disobeyed God and lost his kingdom (1 Samuel 15.1-35). The psalmist says, "Indeed, none who wait for you shall be put to shame; they shall be ashamed who are wantonly treacherous" (Psalm 25.3). Without humility and integrity, there is no loyalty (Psalm 25.21). "Wait for the LORD and keep his way, and he will exalt you" (Psalm 37.34).

4. **I Take Refuge**- "I take refuge in you." (Psalm 25.20)

A refuge is a place of shelter from danger. In Luke 12.13-21, the Rich Fool tried to find security in his money and possessions. When he died, his wealth could not protect him. His well-stocked barns were useless in eternity. Sadly, he trusted his plan and the work of his hands rather than trusting God to take care of Him. Making plans is good, and working hard is important, but relying on God comes first. The safety of the soul comes before the desires of the body. Make your destiny your priority. The proud live for this world. The humble live for heaven. Only God can keep you safe. Take refuge in the Lord.

Avoiding Mistakes

Your children need to know that timidity is not humility (2 Timothy 1.7). Humility is not being shy or unsure. Humble people are confident but not boastful. A person with healthy self-esteem knows their strengths as well as their limitations. Most of all, they know that God deserves the glory for their successes. He guides them and grows them. Life is best when lived with respect for God and your fellow man. Christianity is not a prideful life of self-sufficiency but of humble interdependency.

From beginning to end, Jesus' life and ministry display the majesty of modesty. Teach your child not to be showy or selfish. The humble seek to bless rather than impress. Likable people are down-to-earth. No one likes a know-it-all. A sharp wit is good but making others feel small is bad. Don't be a smart aleck. Others are smart and talented in ways different from you. Value their contributions. Make them feel important. Give them the spotlight. The second greatest command is to love your neighbor as yourself. There is no better guide to humility than this. And when you are genuinely concerned about others, your own life cannot help but improve.

Those who put on an air of superiority, appear snobbish rather than accomplished. The higher you go in life, the more humility is needed. Humble people relate better and achieve more. A big ego is a barrier to friendship and teamwork. Pride isolates you, but humility improves you. Humility facilitates good communication and fosters goodwill. Seek to be useful, not superior. Choose to be helpful, not haughty. James M. Barrie, the author of *Peter Pan*, remarked, "Life is one long lesson in humility." The sooner you learn the lesson, the better life gets.

Practicing the Psalms

To be successful, be correctable.

Text Questions:
1. Name two qualities of God. (Psalm 25.8)
2. Whom does God instruct in the way? (Psalm 25.8)
3. Whom does God lead in what is right? (Psalm 25.9)
4. Name four petitions of the humble. (Psalm 25.5,7,20,18)
5. Name four pledges of the humble. (Psalm 25.1,2,5,20)

Discussion Questions:
1. What is humility?
2. Why is humility attractive?
3. Why is conceit unattractive?
4. What makes a person conceited?
5. What makes a person humble?

Parent/Child Exercise: To help your child understand interdependency, ask them where the things they use come from. Do this throughout the day.

In the morning, begin with everyday items (eggs, bacon, cereal, bananas, plates, cups, spoons, tables, clothes, shoes, refrigerators, cars, pillows, mattresses, windows, shingles, carpet, tile, lamps, faucets, houses, cars, mail, etc.).

In the afternoon, help them to see the cooperation between farmers, harvesters, artisans, packagers, shippers, merchants, advertisers, bankers, educators, and governments.

In the evening, ask them where people come from (moms, dads, aunts, uncles, grandparents, siblings, neighbors, friends, and teachers).

At bedtime, ask them where the sun, moon, stars, and earth come from. In conclusion, recall your earlier conversations and emphasize that everything comes from God (James 1.17).

The point of the exercise is to help them become more grateful and humble. Every person is important. Every person has gifts. Every person is needed. Most of all, we need God who made the world and sustains it by the power of His word. Ask your child how sad it would be if someone did not appreciate other people. And ask how sad it would be if someone thought they did not need God. Let your child tell you why humility is needed to live the best possible life.

Optional Exercise: Have your child blow up a balloon. Ask what happens if you overfill the balloon. Use a sharpie to write the word "ego" on the surface. Discuss the meaning of the word egotism (sense of self-importance). Proverbs 16.18 says, "Pride goes before destruction, and a haughty spirit before a fall." How is an inflated ego like an overinflated balloon? What are the dangers? What is the right amount of self-confidence? Now let all the air out of the balloon. Explain that humility is not a sense of worthlessness (total deflation or self-contempt). Rather, it is appreciating the value of others and affirming the supreme value of God in your life (Mark 12.30). Do not be empty, but do not be overfilled. A lowly spirit is likable and shapable. It allows you to learn and grow as well as to influence and contribute. Think of humility as spiritual balance. Do not look down on others, and do not despise yourself. To keep your balance, love your neighbor as you love yourself (Mark 12.31). That is humility.

Chapter Five
Psalm 27 - Take Courage
Mason Hale

The LORD is my light and my salvation; whom shall I fear? The LORD is the stronghold of my life; of whom shall I be afraid? (Psalm 27.1)

F ear is a natural experience. We can feel threatened by a seemingly infinite number of things. When we see our children experience fear, our protector mode switches on. You take pride in being able to solve problems and fix situations so that your children don't have to experience life's struggles. But here's the real question: What if you can't fix it? What if it's unsolvable? What if you don't have the control, power, or position to make your child's difficulty disappear?

Viktor Frankl, a survivor of Auschwitz, authored a book about the horrors he experienced in the concentration camp. In *Man's Search for Meaning*, he reflected on the despair and powerlessness of his captivity. Frankl noted, "When we are no longer able to change a situation – we are challenged to change ourselves." Imagine David being surrounded by his enemies. His life hangs in the balance. Fear floods his mind and body. The power to change his situation eludes him, but a new thought lifts him. Suddenly, his spirit is elevated out of despair. What is that thought? Where does it come from? How can you harness this spiritual power for yourself? Most importantly, how can you teach your child to unlock this power?

How did David respond to disheartening circumstances? He coped by reminding himself, "The LORD is the stronghold of my life; of whom shall I be afraid?" (Psalm 27.1). David trusted in God as his protector. He believed God was interested in him personally and intimately. David knew the stories of how God helped His people in times of trouble. He protected Abraham when he rescued Lot. He helped Moses deliver Israel from Egypt. The pillar of cloud and fire, parting the Red Sea, and provisions in the wilderness confirmed God's concern for His people.

In verse 3 David declares, "I will be confident." Thoughts can change how you feel; therefore, intentional thoughts give you a degree of control over the way you feel. As a counselor, I'm interested in how people's thoughts influence their behaviors and feelings. I often ask, "what do you tell yourself that gives you permission to feel this way?" We have automatic thoughts that slip past our attention. If a person is perpetually fearful, I regularly hear automatic thoughts that catastrophize situations. These thoughts emphasize one's powerlessness and hopelessness. Read the first three verses of Psalm 27 again. Do you hear David catastrophizing his situation? Does he seem powerless and hopeless? Not at all. What you hear are the intentional thoughts of a man of faith. David replaced the natural thoughts that derive from fear responses with hopeful thoughts prompted by faith. He says: "I will be confident."

How would you feel if your spouse told you repeatedly, "You are confident"? How would you feel if your friends told you that "you are confident"? What about your preacher? Your boss? Yourself? You would feel more confident! Our thoughts have power, especially if they stem from a core belief grounded on the truth of God. What are some promises of God from which you can derive confidence? Consider these passages that illustrate His power and care.

- 2 Corinthians 12.9 "My grace is sufficient for you, for my power is made perfect in weakness."

- Ephesians 6.10 - "Finally, be strong in the Lord and in the strength of his might."

- Isaiah 41.10 - "Fear not, for I am with you; be not dismayed, for I am your God; I will strengthen you, I will help you, I will uphold you with my righteous right hand."

- Isaiah 43.2 - "When you pass through the waters, I will be with you; and through the rivers, they shall not overwhelm you; when you walk through the fire you shall not be burned, and the flame shall not consume you."

Choose the thoughts that you want, and say those thoughts to your child. Your words resonate in the minds of your children. Those words will be repeated when they face trials. Do you want them to be confident? Tell them that you see their confidence and that you see they're capable. Do you want them to be brave? Tell them that you notice their courage. Do you want them to be compassionate with difficult people? Tell them that you see how considerate they are even when that person is difficult.

These opportunities are only available if you are present in the life of your child. You will have to be present in moments when your child can exhibit these qualities for you to notice. The keys to these transformative thoughts are your honesty, transparency, and presence.

This is the posture that God takes with us. He is present in our lives and recognizes our successes and weaknesses. He reminds us that we are loved and assures us we have access to His might amid our powerlessness. These compelling truths are imparted through His Word and His messengers—including you. You can speak these words into your child's heart: "Be strong and courageous. Do not fear or be in dread of them, for it is the LORD your God who goes with you. He will never leave you nor forsake you" (Deuteronomy 31.6). "As for me, I am poor and needy, but the Lord takes thought for me. You are my help and my deliverer" (Psalm 40.17).

Brain Activity During Fear

Fear manifests as a neurological response to external stimuli perceived as a threat. Our minds perceive a threat, activating the sympathetic nervous system. The sympathetic nervous system is responsible for preparing our bodies to survive. We commonly refer to this state as Fight/Flight/Freeze. When the sympathetic nervous system is activated, our bodies redirect focus from less immediately necessary functions like digestion to elevate our heart rate, increase the oxygen absorption rate of our lungs, dilate our eyes, and quickly pump adrenaline through our circulatory system. We are primed to do battle, run away, or stand still depending on the situation.

Once we are in this state, our brains have begun to turn off the executive function of our frontal lobe and pre-frontal cortex, and the emotional center of our brain called the limbic system. Our brain activity ultimately shifts to the brainstem which functions to maintain our survival. If a person is overcome by fear, this is the typical progression that is experienced in the brain.

What we hope for in a healthy brain is for each of these three areas to be active in the presence of fear. We want the logical frontal lobe activated with the emotional limbic system, and the survival-focused brainstem activated and informed by the other systems of the brain. To have each of these three systems activated together one must be able to perceive (1) safety in their environment and (2) safe relational connection. This atmosphere of security and love is experienced in healthy families, churches, and friendships. Most of all, it is perceived in the presence of God.

Safety and Connection

These perceptions of safety are recognizable in Psalm 27. David's belief in God's power provides him with a sense of security in his environment: "The Lord is my light and my salvation; whom shall I fear? The Lord is the stronghold of my life; of whom shall I be afraid?" David imagines God being present in the midst of his enemies. He feels the calming power of God's presence even though he cannot see Him (Hebrews 11.1). David's faith delivers him from fear, but not from his situation.

We want to save our children from fear. We also want desperately to protect our children from pain. We try fervently to change their circumstances to spare them discomfort, but what if we spent our energies building up our children's faith instead? What if we helped them construct a worldview grounded in God's loving presence and providential care? What if we focused on equipping our children with core beliefs that strengthened their faith? What if strengthening their faith was more beneficial than changing their circumstances?

Imagine a world in which your child could face adversity, opposition, and uncertainty with confidence and grace because they have faith that God is beside them in their valley of the shadow of death. Your position as their parent provides the optimal opportunity to instill and solidify these truths by being present and intentional in their life. You have the power to influence the formation of spiritual resilience within your child. Make a difference. Speak life. Instill faith. Overcome fear.

Viktor Frankl wrote, "Everything can be taken from a man but one thing: the last of human freedoms—to choose one's attitude in any given set of circumstances, to choose one's own way." David chose to believe in God and that made all the difference in his life. You can help your child displace unhealthy fear with faith, hope, and love by helping them become more intentional in their thinking.

Paul said, "I can do all things through Christ who strengthens me" (Philippians 4.13). Knowing Christ's power and presence imparts confidence in your ability to face daily difficulties and meet life's demands. It will do the same for your child. Share these words with your son or daughter. Say them together. Memorize them. Pray them. Recite them. Practice them. When the word of Christ dwells in you richly, it improves your thinking and your attitude (Colossians 3.17). Healthier thoughts and affirming attitudes improve your quality of life. By choosing your thoughts you are choosing your future. Train your child to think intentionally and biblically so they can enjoy the best possible life.

Practicing the Psalms

To be successful, unlock your power.

Text Questions:

1. How does "the LORD is my light" apply to experiencing fear? (Psalm 27.1)
2. How does lifting "me high upon a rock" illustrate safety? (Psalm 27.5)
3. What comfort is provided through God hearing your cry? (Psalm 27.7)
4. What benefit is a level path provided by God? (Psalm 27.11)
5. How can waiting on the Lord bring strength to a person? (Psalm 27.14)

Discussion Questions:

1. What do you tell yourself when you are afraid?
2. What thoughts would you rather have?
3. What thoughts would you like your child to have when they are fearful?
4. When will you start telling your child these more helpful thoughts?
5. Why is preparing your child often more important than protecting your child?

Parent/Child Exercise: Repeat these passages together. Read a verse, reflect for one minute, and then share your thoughts and feelings. When finished, discuss how God's word orients your mind. Why is spiritual mindfulness valuable? How is it developed? Who is most responsible for your mindset?

- Romans 8.28 - "And we know that for those who love God all things work together for good, for those who are called according to his purpose."

- Isaiah 60.22 - "I am God. At the right time I'll make it happen." (The Message)

- Psalm 27.14 - "Wait for the LORD: be strong, and let your heart take courage; wait for the LORD!"

- Psalm 34.18 - "The LORD is near to the broken hearted and saves the crushed in spirit."

Chapter Six

Psalm 32 - Shout for Joy

Keith Parker

Many are the sorrows of the wicked, but steadfast love
surrounds the one who trusts in the LORD. Be glad in the
LORD, and rejoice, O righteous, and shout for joy, all you
upright in heart! (Psalm 32.10-11)

If I were to ask you to recite the shortest verse in the Bible,
you probably would say, "Jesus wept." John 11.35 is the
shortest verse in English, but not in the Greek New
Testament. The shortest verse in the original language is not
about crying, it's about rejoicing. Paul wrote in 1
Thessalonians 5.16, "Rejoice always."

I have three children and six grandchildren. Except for my
wife, they are the most important people to me in the world.
As Paul said about the Philippians, my children are the ones
that "I love and long for." They are my pride and joy. More
than anything, I want them to be happy in this life as well as
the next. I want them to experience the shortest verse in the
Bible: Rejoice evermore.

What we want for our children is what God wants for His
children. God wants His kids to be happy. Didn't the
psalmist say, "This is the day that the Lord has made; let us

rejoice and be glad in it" (Psalm 118.24)? And didn't Jesus say, "Rejoice and be glad" (Matthew 5.12)? And didn't Paul write, "Rejoice in the Lord always; again I will say, rejoice" (Philippians 4.4)? And didn't John say, "We are writing these things so that our joy may be complete" (1 John 1.4)? And isn't joy a fruit of the Spirit (Galatians 5.22)? God enthusiastically says from Heaven, "I want my kids to be happy!"

I wish that I could promise you the moon. I wish that I could say, "If you'll just be faithful to Jesus, you will never have any problems." No health problems. No financial problems. No marital problems. No relationship problems. The opposite is true. Christians have problems. Jesus said, "In this world you will have tribulation" (John 16.33). Parents, you may be dealing with the disappointment of a child who tried out for the band, a school play, or the ball team, but didn't make the cut. Maybe your son gave his best effort but failed a test or subject. Maybe your daughter didn't get the job she wanted. Could it be your daughter has broken up with a boyfriend and is feeling rejected? Gloom and despair are in the air. Need a lift? Need a little hope? Need to see your child smile again? Psalm 32 is the answer.

Teach Your Children to Sing

Psalm 32 has a lot to say about joy. The psalm closes with these words: "Rejoice in the Lord and be glad, you righteous; sing, all you who are upright in heart." Do you remember the last time you heard someone sing—outside of church? Perhaps someone in the shower? While driving down the road? At work or school? Or, even in jail? Paul and Silas did. After being beaten and threatened, "about midnight Paul and Silas were praying and singing hymns to God" (Acts 16.25). A singing soul is a joyful soul. "Is anyone cheerful? Let him sing praise" (James 5.13).

Psalm 32 gives us many reasons to sing and rejoice. First, we have been pardoned. Notice how the psalm begins: "Blessed is the one whose transgression is forgiven, whose sin is covered. Blessed is the man against whom the LORD counts no iniquity, and in whose spirit there is no deceit." (Psalm 32.1-2). Regardless of what we as parents have done or have failed to do, we can be forgiven by a gracious God. Regardless of what our children have done—drugs, alcohol, stealing, lying, cursing, sexual immorality—all can be forgiven. There is no sin too big for God's grace. If we die and get to Heaven, we're going to go to Heaven not because we have been so good to Jesus. We will get to Heaven because Jesus has been so good to us. Thank God for His forgiveness!

Teach Your Children to Pray

Second, God has given us prayer. "Therefore let everyone who is godly offer prayer to you" (Psalm 32.6). Imagine that you have access to some of the world's greatest leaders. What if you had the phone number of the President of the

United States? Anytime you want, you can call the President to seek his advice, ask for wisdom, or just talk about anything going on in your life. Well, I don't know the phone number of the President, but I can give you the number of the one who created the President. Would you like God's phone number? Here it is: 333. Or more specifically, Jeremiah 33.3. "Call to me, and I will answer you."

Answer this question: My family and I share a prayer…

A.   Every day.
B.   Sometimes.
C.   Very seldom.
D.   Not at all.

I've asked that question all across America. Ninety percent of the time the number one answer is C and the number two answer is D. Except for meal-time prayers, we very seldom or never pray with our families. Acts 21.5 serves as a great example for families: "When our days there were ended, we departed and went on our journey, and they all, with wives and children, accompanied us until we were outside the city. And kneeling down on the beach, we prayed." You've heard it many times, "Families that pray together, stay together." Call to God and He will answer.

Teach Your Children to Trust God

Third, we have His presence. God indeed is our "hiding place" (Psalm 32.7). Jesus promised His disciples, "I am with you always" (Matthew 28.20). Moses promised Israel, "Be strong and courageous...for it is the LORD your God who goes with you. He will not leave you or forsake you." (Deuteronomy 31.6).

When we became Christians, God not only gave us the forgiveness of sins but also His abiding presence in the gift of the Holy Spirit (Acts 2.38). Our bodies are the temple or home of God's Spirit (1 Corinthians 6.19). That's one of the reasons we should encourage our teenagers to remain sexually pure. "Flee from sexual immorality" (1 Corinthians 6.18). Why? Because God lives in our bodies. How beautiful is the thought, "In your presence there is fullness of joy" (Psalm 16.11)!

Teach Your Children to Be Brave

Fourth, God has given us His protection. The psalmist said, "You preserve me from trouble" (Psalm 32.7). Parents, please be aware of the dangers of peers who seek to blast and belittle. Maybe there is someone older or stronger who is upsetting your children or picking on them at school. One of the rising problems in our world is cyberbullying. Threats are made and words are spoken that are intended to scare, manipulate, or destroy. Keep reminding your little ones that they should tell you when anything like this is taking place. Also, remind them that God will fight their battles and "they will be protected forever" (Psalm 37.28).

Teach Your Children to Seek Wisdom

Fifth, we have God's precepts. "I will instruct you and teach you in the way you should go" (Psalm 32.8). The longest psalm (chapter) in the Bible is Psalm 119. And the whole psalm speaks of God's commands, teachings, and precepts. From this psalm, we learn that his precepts are to be obeyed (4), meditated upon (15), understood (27), longed for (40), sought out (45), followed (63), kept (69), considered (128), loved (159) and chosen (173).

Dads and moms, let me encourage you to be like the people of Berea (Acts 17.11). They searched the scriptures every day. We make sure that our children are fed physically. Make sure your children are fed spiritually. We are diligent in making sure that they get their homework. Make sure that they get their "heaven work."

Sit down with your children after dinner and read the Bible together. Read the Proverbs. Proverbs has 31 chapters. In the months that have 31 days, read a chapter a day. There are 150 Psalms. In the months that have 30 days, read 5 Psalms every day, and you'll be blessed by reading the whole book in a month. The psalmist put it like this in Psalm 119.11: "I have stored up your word in my heart, that I might not sin against you." God's word will keep us from sin and sin will keep us from God's word.

Teach Your Children to Love

Sixth, we have God's passion. "Many are the sorrows of the wicked, but steadfast love surrounds the one who trusts in the LORD." (Psalm 32.10). Our children need to know that "The LORD is merciful and gracious, slow to anger and abounding in steadfast love" (Psalm 103.8). Our children need to know that "as a father shows compassion to His children, so the Lord shows compassion to those who fear him" (Psalm 103.13). There is nothing that our children can do to make us quit loving them. And there is nothing that we can do to stop the passion of God (Romans 8.38-39).

We, like God, must be people of love. We must be servants of God and others. In Philippians 2.1-5 Paul speaks about the "joy" that comes from loving God and others.

> So if there is any encouragement in Christ, any comfort from love, any participation in the Spirit, any affection and sympathy, [2] complete my **joy** by being of the same mind, having the same love, being in full accord and of one mind. [3] Do nothing from selfish ambition or conceit, but in humility count others more significant than **yourselves**. [4] Let each of you look not only to his own interests, but also to the interests

of **others**. [5] Have this mind among yourselves, which is yours in Christ **Jesus**, [emphasis mine]

The last word in verse 5 is "Jesus." The last word in verse 4 is "others." And the last word in verse 3 is "yourselves." Do you want to have joy? Let the "J" stand for "Jesus." Let the "O" stand for "others." Let the "Y" stand for "Yourselves." The way to have joy—put Jesus first, others second, and yourself third.

Restoring Joy

As you can imagine, Psalm 32 can be used to help our children in many situations. If your children are feeling guilty because they disobeyed something that you asked them to do, restore joy to their spirit by taking them to the first few verses of this psalm. Remind them of the pardon that both you and God offer.

If your teenager is uncertain about which university to attend or which job to choose, remind him of the wisdom that God gives through prayer. "Ask, and it shall be given to you" (Matthew 7.7). If there is sadness because of the rejection of a friend, reassure your children that God will never forsake us (Hebrews 13.5). His presence is lasting.

Growing up as a kid, I played pee-wee football and wore the number 32. I treasure the memories of those days. Want good memories? Treasure Psalm 32. Listen to it. Learn it. Love it. And live it. Psalm 32 will put a song in your heart, a leap in your step, and a smile on your face.

Practicing the Psalms

To be successful, live joyfully.

Text Questions:

1. What is the Bible's shortest verse? Why is it important?
2. How did Paul and Silas respond when facing trouble?
3. Who has the privilege of prayer? (Psalm 32.6)
4. How often did the Bereans search the scriptures?
5. Who is blessed according to Psalm 32.1?

Discussion Questions:

1. When is it appropriate to confess to others?
2. Why is confession hard?
3. Is there any sin that God will not forgive? If so, explain.
4. Using Psalm 119, list some blessings of Bible study.
5. When are you the happiest? What makes you happy?
6. How can putting yourself last result in joy?

Parent/Child Exercise: Bake cookies for someone who would least expect it. Deliver them with a card expressing your love and appreciation. Observe any joyful response from the recipient. How did this kind gesture make you feel?

Chapter Seven

Psalm 37 - Fret Not

Don Loftis

Fret not yourself because of evildoers; be not envious of wrongdoers! For they will soon fade like the grass and wither like the green herb. Trust in the LORD, and do good; dwell in the land and befriend faithfulness. Delight yourself in the LORD, and he will give you the desires of your heart. Commit your way to the LORD; trust in him, and he will act. He will bring forth your righteousness as the light, and your justice as the noonday. Be still before the LORD and wait patiently for him; fret not yourself over the one who prospers in his way, over the man who carries out evil devices! (Psalm 37.1-7)

Have you ever had one of those days where everything seemed to go wrong? The alarm didn't go off, traffic was slow, the boss was in a bad mood, and you started a fever blister. On top of it, everybody else seemed to be having a great day – no problems, or so it seemed.

Life is like that sometimes—a "bummer" at best, unfair at worst. David had been anointed to take the place of Saul, the ungodly king who consistently disobeyed Jehovah. However, it was David who constantly had to flee for his life and live like a fugitive. In contemplating those injustices, he wrote Psalm 37. In the opening verses, he described his plan for dealing with life's unfairness. He wrote, "Trust in the Lord" (3), "Do good" (3), "Delight yourself in the Lord" (4), "Commit your way to the Lord" (5), and "Be still before the Lord and wait patiently" (7). These strategies worked for David, and they will work for you.

In this lesson, we are especially concerned with envy because it is the enemy of gratitude and contentment. Envy is choosing a negative response to life's confrontations. It is defined as a feeling of displeasure and distress at learning about another's blessings. The ancient Greek philosopher, Plato, listed envy as a "pain of the soul" and the Holy Spirit put it in the list of "the works of the flesh" in Galatians 5.21.

It was Cain's envy of his brother's acceptance by the Lord that led him to commit murder. 1 John 3.12 makes that clear: "We should not be like Cain, who was of the evil one and murdered his brother. And why did he murder him? Because his own deeds were evil and his brother's righteous." Joseph's brothers hated him and sold him as a slave, because of their father's favoritism toward Joseph. The same dangers are exposed in Korah's rebellion against Moses (Numbers 16.1-3), Haman's plots against Mordecai (Esther 6), and even the crucifixion of Jesus. Pilate knew that "it was out of envy that they had delivered him up" (Matthew 27.18).

Envy is a dangerous emotion that leads to bitterness, hate, and revenge. It sabotages personal happiness and pushes us away from the heart of Jesus. The writer of Proverbs accurately stated, "A tranquil heart gives life to the flesh, but envy makes the bones rot" (Proverbs 14.30). The apostle Peter wrote, "So put away all malice and all deceit and hypocrisy and envy and all slander" (I Peter 2.1), and Paul added, "love does not envy" (1 Corinthians 13.4). True love and envy are incompatible.

Understanding Envy in Children

Adults frequently deal with attitudes of envy. We observe those whose lives seem easier or whose incomes appear higher, and we wonder "why not us?" Friendships and marriages can be ruined by jealousy or competition.

Yet, it would be a mistake to think that our children do not encounter feelings of envy in their lives. A younger sibling may be jealous of the freedoms an older brother or sister is allowed. Children may feel threatened by a new baby or a new parental relationship. Failure to excel in academics or to win the starting role on a sports team may create bad feelings toward peers. Like adults, children can be overly impressed by houses, cars, vacations, clothes, or attention.

In reality, the young struggle more with envy because of limited life experience. Small things become big, and temporary issues seem permanent. They may fail to move past these feelings and may even transfer negative feelings to others. Some research suggests that teenagers can demonstrate anger towards parents because of the perceived unfairness that they experience elsewhere. Mom or dad can become a convenient target of negative feelings that originate at school or in the neighborhood.

Developing a Strategy

Psalm 37 addresses the mature approach to life's issues. Faith, patience, and service are great skills to help you put an end to envy. How can we communicate these values to our children? There are many avenues, but let's examine four.

Strategy #1 - Teach Your Children to Count Their Blessings.

First, help your children recognize their blessings. The more we look at the good things in our lives, the greater our level of contentment. Similarly, the more we gaze at the things of others, the greater the likelihood of discontent and envy. Where we focus our attention is a choice.

Are you familiar with the 80-20 rule? It suggests that if we spend 80% of our time looking at the 20% that is not great, we will conclude that 80% of our life is bad. In a similar way, even if we are going through a difficult time, spending 80% of our time contemplating the 20% that is good will result in feeling greatly blessed. The formula simply reminds us that happiness in life is dominated by the things about which we choose to think.

Thanksgiving is taught by example. As adults, do we complain about our job? Do we gripe about the government? Do we criticize the church? What portion of our prayers are devoted to giving thanks in comparison to making requests? A child's view of the world is shaped by what he or she sees and hears, so model gratitude.

Sharing with others is another great way to cultivate a spirit of appreciation. When you give, you bless others, but you are blessed at the same time. Jesus taught, "It is more blessed to give than to receive" (Acts 20.35). Have your children join you in small but frequent acts of service. They will enjoy and look forward to these times together.

Strategy #2 - Teach Your Children to Celebrate Others' Successes.

Secondly, envy is eliminated when we celebrate the victories and successes of others. Paul challenged the Christians in Rome to "Rejoice with those who rejoice, weep with those who weep." Why is it that many find it easier to commiserate with those who are hurting than to celebrate with those who are rejoicing? That is especially true if their rejoicing was at the expense of our team or our advancement.

We live in a culture of competition. This is evident in athletics, politics, and job advancement. There is great emphasis on personal rights with little talk of personal sacrifice. Paul challenged the Christians in Corinth, "Let no one seek his own good, but the good of his neighbor." Disciples of Christ of all ages are called to prize and practice teamwork rather than competition.

Jesus shared a parable about several day laborers who were hired during the grape harvest. Some worked a full day, others just one hour. At the close of the day, each man received a denarius – the standard wage for a full day's work. Those who had worked longer thought this generosity was unfair and grumbled at the vineyard owner. The owner replied, "Friend, I am doing you no wrong. Did you not agree with me for a denarius? Take what belongs to you and go. I choose to give to this last worker as I give to you. Am I not allowed to do what I choose with what belongs to me? Or do you begrudge my generosity?" (Matthew 20.13b-15). Not *everyone* can win, but we can *all* rejoice with the winner. Personal disappointment does not have to lead to envy.

Strategy #3 - Teach Your Children To Evaluate Price Tags.

A third strategy involves recognizing price tags. When a wise shopper finds the perfect dress or suit, the next thing they do is look at the price tag. What does it cost? Is it really worth it? Often the "blessing" that a neighbor receives comes with a hidden cost that we never considered. The new promotion may require 65 hours a week or a lot of travel. The new house or car requires payments that create debt and marital discord. These dangers are magnified if the apparent benefit reduces the recipient's spiritual focus.

The grass often seems greener on the other side, but appearances can be deceiving. Do you recall the Greek myth about King Midas? This greedy ruler of Phrygia was granted one wish. Despite warnings, he chose to have everything he touched turn to gold. That was fine when he touched a table or carpet or even a rose. However, golden toast and golden grapes were hard to digest. The ultimate tragedy came as he hugged his little daughter, and she became a golden statue. We should be cautious in reacting to the good fortune of others; we don't really know its hidden cost. Helping youngsters to properly evaluate life's price tags is a key component to their maturity.

Strategy #4 - Teach Your Children They Are Valuable.

Finally, we can help our children overcome envy and jealousy by sensing their uniqueness. There is nothing wrong with having models or individuals we aspire to emulate. However, every individual possesses unique talents and opportunities. Joshua could learn from Moses, but he was never intended to be Moses. Some sense a measure of envy on the part of Peter, as he observed John's relationship with Jesus. Peter was not called to be John; he was simply to be a disciple of Jesus.

Helping children discover their worth within a family and within God's kingdom is crucial to their healthy development. When we feel valued, we feel secure. When we feel useful, we feel competent. Remember, contentment is a great antidote to envy.

Conclusion

Since envy is a universal emotion, it does no good for parents to deny its existence. Likewise, punishing a child for expressing these feelings only increases the problem. The goal is to help our children deal with these feelings. In the process, they will develop more gratitude and enjoy more contentment.

Practicing the Psalms

To be successful, count your blessings.

Text Questions:

1. What should God's people not fret about?
2. Evildoers will fade like what?
3. Believers should trust in the Lord and do what?
4. What will God give those who delight in Him?
5. What will God bring forth like light?

Discussion Questions:

1. What is envy? What are its consequences?
2. How did David respond when treated unfairly?
3. Can you offer examples of envy in the Scriptures?
4. When have you experienced envy In your own life?
5. Is it easier to weep with those who weep or rejoice with those who rejoice? Why?

Parent/Child Exercises:

1. *Strategy #1 Exercise* - Frequently, we need to have our children make a list of their blessings. That may be a thanksgiving journal, a special time of prayer, or even a youth group activity. The songwriter was right: "Count your many blessings, name them one by one. And it will surprise you what the Lord has done."
2. *Strategy #2 Exercise* - When something good happens to someone, we need to involve our children in celebrating that blessing. It might be inviting a family over for a celebratory meal, sending congratulatory cards, or praying aloud for these people. Sportsmanship needs to be praised more than winning.

3. *Strategy #3 Exercise* - With older children, it might be useful to look at the price tags of success. Help your youngsters to have fair evaluations of the good fortune of others. Tell the story of King Midas, and have them share what they think would be the worst consequence of this apparent blessing.

4. *Strategy #4 Exercise* - The next time one of your children says, "I wish I was like…" or "I wish I could …," sit down together and help them list their unique traits, abilities, and passions. If there are siblings, it might be useful to have them assist in the list.

Chapter Eight

Psalm 46 - Be Still and Know

Dale Jenkins

God is our refuge and strength, a very present help in trouble. Therefore we will not fear though the earth gives way, though the mountains be moved into the heart of the sea, though its waters roar and foam, though the mountains tremble at its swelling. Selah. *There is a river whose streams make glad the city of God, the holy habitation of the Most High. God is in the midst of her; she shall not be moved; God will help her when morning dawns. The nations rage, the kingdoms totter; he utters his voice, the earth melts. The LORD of hosts is with us; the God of Jacob is our fortress.* Selah. *Come, behold the works of the LORD, how he has brought desolations on the earth. He makes wars cease to the end of the earth; he breaks the bow and shatters the spear; he burns the chariots with fire. "Be still, and know that I am God. I will be exalted among the nations, I will be exalted in the earth!" The LORD of hosts is with us; the God of Jacob is our fortress.* Selah. *(Psalm 46.1-11)*

Imagine your child wants to learn to swim but has a fear of the water. You sign them up for a swim lesson or two. When you book the class, the instructor you select lists that she has been teaching children to swim for over 20 years and has a 3-month waiting list to get into her classes.

She has taught over 2500 children to swim and has a 97% excellent rating from her students. On the day of the first session, the teacher greets your child with kindness and assurance that she will help them love the water. Her focus is on your child. She is down on their level and talking to them with excitement. How would they feel about that teacher? How would they feel about their capability. Like a good coach, you can help your children grow in confidence.

Confidence can be a thing of beauty that helps children achieve and succeed. However, false or misplaced confidence can destroy a child's spirit. God wants His children to enjoy the calm and positive waters that come from placing our confidence in Him. His Word provides plenty of evidence to help your child trust in Him. It can also help you assist them in establishing that spiritual trait in their character.

A Personal Journey

My wife and I were blessed with two sons, so it won't surprise you that we took special note of families ahead of us in the parenting journey that also had two sons. We watched to see what we could learn, and we learned a lot. In our congregation, two families stood out to me. We'll call one set of sons Andy and James and the other set Jody and Brad (obviously not their real names). Both sets of parents were faithful, active, and deeply engaged servants. But as the two sets of sons grew up, I began to notice one set struggling and the other set flourishing. What was the difference?

It took me a long time to put my finger on it, but I'm pretty certain I discovered the difference, and I want to share it with you. It is a quality vital for effectiveness in life. Once identified, I strove to instill it in my sons. The missing ingredient in Andy and James—that was evident in Jody and Brad—was CONFIDENCE.

What is the Definition of Confidence?

Webster lists three meanings for confidence:

>   1. A consciousness of one's powers.

>   2. The quality of being certain.

>   3. A trust or a secret shared.

"Confidence" is a word that is easier to define than possess. This trait can be very elusive. Many children start well, but somewhere along the way, they lose it. Perhaps the world is constantly disturbing the calm waters that confidence brings. By the time they hit maturity, your child will have heard "you can't," "you're not good enough," and "you're too small/young/fat/inexperienced" so often it would be easy to drown in the deep end of the confidence pool.

Instilling confidence in your children can be very deceptive. Let me explain what I mean. If you google: "How do I infuse a child with confidence?" the answers will be pretty consistent:

1. Model confidence in yourself—even if you're not quite feeling it!
2. Don't get upset about their mistakes.
3. Encourage them to try new things.
4. Allow them to fail.
5. Give them balanced feedback.
6. Praise perseverance.
7. Help them find their passion.
8. Set goals.
9. Teach them to talk themselves up.
10. Help them find a hobby.

As you work through your search results, the lists and principles are basically the same. They are about pumping your child full of feel-good principles about themselves regardless of the actions they take.

Be aware that this is a setup for failure. Don't get me wrong. There are some good ideas in each list. However, it doesn't take an advanced degree for your child to know when they've failed. They know their strengths and weaknesses. If their confidence is baseless, what happens when they experience massive failure? While some will find a proper balance, many will spend most of their lives kicking themselves. Others will become so narcissistic that they destroy their successes and become impossible for future spouses, employers, and friends to endure.

In a culture super-infused with "you can do/be/have anything you want" it is not shocking that so many attempt, fail, and then become despondent, or worse. It is not surprising that we have rampant suicide, cutting, and other self-harm incidents. We pump them full of pseudo-self-confidence, and then send them out into a world that quickly punctures that balloon with the pin of reality. The truth is that they do have shortcomings, and they need to adapt accordingly. The truth is that people who tell them otherwise may be using them as a stepping stone. The truth is that someone else is more talented or better equipped in some areas. No child is capable in all things, and it is not hurtful for them to assess their limitations as well as their gifts.

The Apostle Paul referred to a very unhealthy mentality in Philippians 3.3-4. He calls it, "confidence in the flesh": "For it is we who are the circumcision, we who serve God by his Spirit, who boast in Christ Jesus, and who put no confidence in the flesh—though I myself have reasons for such confidence" (Philippians 3.3-4). In rapid-fire style, he lists his super impressive laundry list of "confidence in the flesh" credentials. Then, in verses 7-11, Paul says he found a better way.

Recently, I heard a preacher who suggested that one of the most dangerous words in the dictionary is the word "self." He spoke of some of the ways we use this word: "self-esteem," "self-awareness," "self-importance," "self-help," "self-gratification," and "self-consciousness." You get the picture. If I remember correctly, he said there are more than 300 "self" words in the English language!

How do you get your child through the challenging moments when life is the most fear-inducing? Two lessons are critical. First, take your focus away from yourself. Second place your focus on God the Father, the Son, and the Spirit. When you do this, you have a better chance to overcome. To say it simply: We need more God-consciousness and less self-consciousness. For this lesson let's go to Psalm 46 where you will discover some confidence builders you can share with your child.

Three Confidence Builders

1. Know that "God is!"

No Christian parent will be surprised to learn that the result of taking God out of the school systems, the media, and the state house has resulted in the deterioration of the family and society. Crime has escalated, and neighborliness has declined. As your child faces anxiety propelled by growing apathy and incivility, repeating these two words can give them the confidence to face it all: "God is."

2. Know that God is "a very present help."

Teach your child that God is present and helpful. He is not a distant Being on a far-off planet, but neither is He a traffic cop waiting to find your child at fault. God is your child's heavenly Father, and He has both the ability and the will to help them.

3. Know that God is a very present help when you are "in trouble."

Help your child to understand that God's timing is sometimes different from ours because He knows more than we do. He sees the whole picture. We only see a small part. Trust His timing!

Fear Busters

The psalmist concludes, "Therefore: We will not fear, though the earth be removed, And though the mountains be carried into the midst of the sea; Though its waters roar and be troubled, Though the mountains shake with its swelling." Teach your child that God is bigger than the scariest thing they will ever face. Confidence is grounded on faith in God. You can trust God even though…

- You wake up on the day of a big event with a big pimple.
- Your enemy seeks to embarrass you.
- You are walking into a big scary new school.
- You feel like a complete outsider.
- Your whole world feels out of control.

Was it ingrained in you that good parents should teach their children they can do or be anything? Some well-meaning but misguided adviser may have told you, "Philippians 4.13 says, 'I can do all things through Christ who strengthens me.'" The confidence Paul is talking about is not that you are invincible. He is not saying, "Don't worry, you may be 5 foot 3 and unathletic, but if you try hard, you can play for the Lakers someday." He is saying that you can be confident that you can face whatever you go against, including occasional disappointment (Philippians 4.12; 1 Corinthians 10.13).

The better course is to help your child (1) learn what they can do and (2) discover what they love to do. Help them to find their place in God's plan. 1 Corinthians 12.18 says it well: "God arranged the members in the body, each one of them, as he chose." Don't limit your child's dreams, but help them discern the best fit. Godly parents help their children strive to become the best *they* can be!

Parents, we need to understand and model this so our children can taste it. Children learn in many ways: reading, listening, watching, and experiencing. Sometimes, the most powerful way of learning is the immersive experience of living in your presence. The great news is that you can do this and are not alone in it. You have friends who are attempting to model the same values. You have a church full of those who have done it. And you have God who is "a very present help."

We sing a song from Psalm 46 that says the "God of angel armies" watches over us (7). Verses 4-9 give us a glimpse of the power of God over the powers of the earth. When your child feels outnumbered, have them read these verses. Then share Psalm 27.3 with them: "Though an army encamp against me, my heart shall not fear; though war arise against me, yet I will be confident."

Proverbs 3.25-26 says, "Do not be afraid of sudden terror or of the ruin of the wicked, when it comes, for the Lord will be your confidence and will keep your foot from being caught." Talk to your children honestly about the source of real confidence. Real confidence is not chest-thumping arrogance. Rather, it is knowing that "the Lord will be your confidence."

One writer paraphrases Psalm 46.10, "Step out of the traffic! Take a long, loving look at me, your High God, above politics, above everything" (MSG). While I'm not always a fan of that particular paraphrase, I do appreciate the idea that God transcends the politics of our current culture. When your children are told that they are "on the wrong side of history," they need to be reminded that our God is above social trends in politics. Verse 10 is the key to building real confidence: "He says, 'Be still, and know that I am God; I will be exalted among the nations, I will be exalted in the earth.'"

If one thing is most descriptive of the 21st century, it is noise. EarPods, cell phones, social media, and talking heads are ever-present. Noise is everywhere. There is so much noise that we might miss God's "voice" amid our worries. Help your child to learn to disconnect from electronics and experience the calming power of meditating on God's word. By helping them get to know God's presence, power, and promises, you can build appropriate confidence in the heart of your children.

Practicing the Psalms

To be successful, ignore the noise.

Text questions:
1. Who is our refuge and strength? (46.1)
2. When is God a very present help? (46.1)
3. If the earth gives way, what will believers not do? (46.2)
4. What helpful thing can you do to know God? (46.10)
5. Where will God be exalted? (46.10)

Discussion questions:
1. Discuss and write down a workable, age-appropriate definition of "confidence."
2. Have each family member share times when their confidence shrinks.
3. Discuss the value of worship as a focusing place in a disordered world.
4. What else can you do to remind yourself of God's care when your world is shaking?
5. Have each family member share places they go to when facing anxiety.

Parent/Child Exercise: Use your Bible app or computer and search various translations for the word "confidence." Make 10 3x5 cards with "confidence" verses on them and place them in strategic places, e.g., car dashboard, bathroom mirror, refrigerator door, etc.

Chapter Nine

Psalm 51 - Sing Out Loud

Neal Pollard

Have mercy on me, O God, according to your steadfast love;
according to your abundant mercy blot out my
transgressions. (Psalm 51.1)

A t different ages and stages, children disobey God's law while in our homes. Knowing this, we must prepare ourselves to handle these seminal moments in their growth and development. It is hard to convey the heartaches that accompany the choice to sin against God and others. At times we have walked that painful road ourselves. Often we have seen others suffer the painful consequences of disobedience. Occasionally we have witnessed the heartbreak of other parents in similar circumstances. Sooner or later, we will likely come face to face with the failures of our sons and daughters. Broken and disillusioned, they may come to us weary from the burden of sin and its effects. What we say and do next is extremely important!

Some psalms refer to events from Israel's early history, but other psalms were written in response to recent happenings. Of the latter category, none is more notable than Psalm 51. Your Bible may have a heading like this: "For the choir director. A Psalm of David, when Nathan the prophet came to him after he had gone in to Bathsheba." This refers to the events in 2 Samuel 12.1-15 when Nathan confronted David with his sin using these unforgettable words: "You are the man!" Despite David's despicable actions involving Uriah and Bathsheba, this psalm shows us why he is a man after God's own heart (1 Samuel 13.14; Acts 13.22). He endured serious consequences for these sins, but he also models the way forward through the penitent words in this Psalm. Our children will need those inspired words many times in their lives.

Acknowledge What You Have Done

Notice that David's attitude is not, "If I have offended anyone, I'm sorry." He's not defensive, proud, or self-excusing. He lays his heart bare before God's all-seeing eyes. Frankly and freely, he confesses his sin. In Psalm 51, he calls his actions by five names:

Transgressions - Crimes or offenses (1,3).

Iniquity - To bend, twist, or deviate from the way (2,5,9).

Sin - To miss the mark, do wrong, or offend (2,3,5,9).

Evil - To do bad, to treat badly (4).

Bloodguiltiness - Guilt due to murder or bloodshed (14).

Spiritual healing is impossible without honestly facing our past. David knew what he had done, and his sin was "ever" before him (3). Please note that it should not remain this way, but it must start this way. Godly sorrow comes first. The joy of forgiveness follows.

Understand What God Can Do

Many people imitate David's first step (remorse) but never move beyond it to take the next step (repentance). Satan is pleased for us to come to grips with the *reality* of our sins, but he doesn't want us to come to grips with the *remedy* for our sins. David is determined to get past this, and he realizes that God is the key. David does two noteworthy things in this penitent poem. First, he celebrates God's forgiving nature: His "steadfast love" (1), "mercy" (1), "righteousness" (14), and "good pleasure" (18). Second, he repeatedly pleads for God to forgive him:

- "Have mercy on me" (1)
- "Wash me thoroughly" (2,7)
- "Cleanse me" (2)
- "Purge me with hyssop" (7)
- "Let me hear joy and gladness" (8)
- "Create in me a clean heart" (10)
- "Renew a right spirit within me" (10)
- "Cast me not away from your presence" (11)

- "Take not your Holy Spirit from me" (11)
- "Restore to me the joy of your salvation" (12)
- "Uphold me" (12)
- "Deliver me" (14)
- "Open my lips" (15)

The focus of this psalm is on God's power to forgive and heal. How often do we doubt God's willingness to restore us and make us whole again? Consequently, we stay stuck in remembrance of our guilt rather than relying on God's grace to help us rise above our past.

Do What You Must Do

When we move past sin and return to serving God, our daily "to-do" list is transformed. Purposing to do better is the right response. David tells us what he wants to do in moving past his awful past. Notice how David is forward-thinking and full of resolve. He uses words like "then I will" (13) and "I shall be" (7). Think about your sinful past. How does it compare to David's? Or Peter's? Or Paul's? Each of these men refused to be defined by their past. Instead, they depended on their prospects. Fruits of repentance are indications of an inward change. These selfless acts are the result of a broken spirit and a contrite heart (17). Inward change produces outward change.

Help Others Do What They Should Do

David understood that at some point he needed to broaden his focus. Being restored to God's favor involves helping others who are in need. David could have convinced himself that he was no good to God anymore because of his sin. Who would listen to him? Who could benefit from his words and encouragement? But notice verses 13-19. They are all about his mission among others. We are healed to help others who need healing. This understanding is vital to God's process of reconciliation.

David was broken and battered by sin. He would feel its effects in his public life and his private life for the rest of his days. In the aftermath of his affair with Bathsheba and the subsequent cover-up, the wounds of sin left visible scars. With Nathan's words ringing in his ears, he sits down to pen the haunting but hopeful 51st Psalm. We often dwell more on the first part—the multifaceted description of sin and the marvelous pictures of forgiveness—but to me, the most beautiful part of the psalm is when David uses the word "then."

Satan would love for sin to defeat us. He would like our feelings of guilt to overwhelm us and keep us from the wonderful restoration David experienced. David speaks prospectively when he asks for a clean heart, renewed spirit, fellowship, joy, and sustenance from God. He asks for these things with a purpose in mind. This part of the Psalm often gets neglected. Consider a few practical applications that you can practice and pass on to your children. What does God want after our "cuts" become "scars"?

After Cuts Become Scars

Reach out to the lost. (Psalm 51.13)

On the other side of repentance, David was anxious to help others reeling from their spiritual wounds. As we overcome sin with God's help, we can be a tool in His hand to rescue others who struggle just as we did. It would be better not to have gone down the road of sin, but having come back, we can understand the desperation of those longing for restoration. Knowledge of the way back and assurance that there is a way back, are some of the most precious gifts you will ever give to your child.

Be a faithful worshipper. (Psalm 51.14)

David, the master musician, lost his song in the far country. He yearned for the joyful singing he remembered. When we are living in darkness, worship loses its power and purity. We feel hypocritical and empty as we go through the motions. When we return to His glorious light, we experience that lifted-up feeling once more. David shows us the blessing of restoration. The joy of a renewed spirit is enhanced in faithful worship.

Give God sacrifices. (Psalm 51.15-17)

More than ever, David understood that the sacrifices God
most wants are a broken spirit and a contrite heart. These
sacrifices reveal themselves in service to others. This is not
a guilt-driven service but a gratitude-driven service. Having
been made whole, David better appreciates what God
wants from him and for him. The point is that we can be
fruitful and useful to Him, scars and all.

Accept God's delight. (Psalm 51.18-19)

How many times did David relive that rooftop moment and
the regrettable sins that followed? How often did he wish he
could just go back and undo it all? How long did he wrestle
with accepting God's forgiveness and wondering if God
could take him back? These longings reveal David's
hopefulness about the prospect of God's delight.

He feels a responsibility to help others, and he wants to
encourage them to do what's right—but I love what he
anticipates will be the outcome of these heartfelt endeavors.
He knows that God will be delighted with the offering. Did
you know that? Did you know that God can delight in you
again when you bring Him your sin-scarred life and offer
Him your righteous sacrifices? He doesn't want to discard
you. He wants to delight in you!

David could not undo his past, but he did the right thing. Having dealt with his past, he focused on the present and looked to the future. That is what God wants your child to do after cuts become scars!

Practicing the Psalms

To be successful, use your scars.

Text Questions:
1. What words does David use to describe sin?
2. How does he describe God's response to repentance?
3. How does David speak of his new future?
4. What does David anticipate doing going forward?
5. Why would he turn his focus to others after benefitting from God's mercy?

Discussion Questions:
1. Why are some sins harder to overcome?
2. What keeps us from putting it behind us?
3. Which metaphor for healing do you relate to most?
4. How can we help our children understand God's grace?
5. Do you think it is wise to disclose your past sins and failures with your child as a means of helping them work through their sin problems? Why or why not?

Parent/Child Exercise: Purchase a hyssop plant or some hyssop oil. Research the medicinal properties of hyssop and then explain them to your child using the hyssop as an object lesson. Discuss how the application of God's mercy to our spiritual and emotional wounds is comparable to hyssop.

Chapter Ten

Psalm 90 - Number Your Days

Aubrey Johnson

Your children are counting on you to provide them with the knowledge and wisdom they need to live successfully. One thing they need from you is an understanding of time and its meaning in their lives. Life at its essence is time—the progress of events from birth to death—but earth-time does not tell the whole story of one's life. It is only the first phase.

Your child needs to know that heaven-time coexists with earth-time, but each pertains to a different realm of reality. Earth-time refers to time lived in the physical body as a home for the human spirit. The body's five senses limit your perception to the present world, but faith enables you to perceive what currently exists beyond this world (Romans 10.17). A better and longer life awaits you.

It is helpful to view death as transitional rather than terminal. Rather than morbid, thoughts of death should be motivational. Death is not the end of life. It is merely the end of life in this realm. Those who understand this make the most of their days on earth and look forward to the joys of heaven. They are more peaceful and purposeful. Death is a point of departure rather than a dead-end. One of the best things about heaven-time is that it never ends.

So what do your children need to know about time? In Psalm 90, Moses shares three essentials loving parents can impart to the next generation: life is (1) brief, (2) observed, and (3) spent. When you know your life is *brief*, you don't want to waste a minute. When you know your life is *observed*, you want to use it to please your heavenly Father. When you know your life is *spent*, you want to use it wisely rather than foolishly. Children who understand these truths have a distinct advantage over those who don't.

Life Is Brief - *Read Psalm 90.1-6 with your child.*

Talk with your child about America's great mountain ranges. The Smokies and Rockies were here before you were born, and will continue after you are gone. Mountains are older than trees, but the world is older than mountains. The earth looked different before earthquakes and eruptions formed today's mountain ranges.

Ask your child if they know what is older than trees, mountains, or planets. Before the earth was formed, God always existed. He has been here in every generation from Adam to the present day. And since he made the world and all its inhabitants, you could say that He is our dwelling place. We dwell in bodies He made, on a planet He created, and in families He designed. Without God, you would have no existence or place in which to exist.

Imagine Forever

Moses described God as everlasting. Everlasting is a long time. It is hard to imagine forever. Trees die, rocks erode, and planets perish, but God is endless. He was here before the universe was formed, and He will be here after it is gone. He is spirit rather than flesh, indestructible rather than corruptible, and eternal rather than temporary.

Humans have a limited earthly life span. Human bodies decompose and return to dust. When your heart stops beating, your body dies, but your spirit does not die. It returns to God. In Ecclesiastes, Solomon compared physical death to four manmade objects reaching their useful end: a silver cord that snaps; a golden bowl that breaks; a water pitcher that shatters; and a cistern wheel that stops working (Ecclesiastes 12.6).

These examples make a single point. Just as material objects break down over time, so does the human body. Solomon uses silver and gold to illustrate the preciousness of life. The unique design and purpose of each item suggest that every person is divinely gifted and has a God-given purpose (1 Peter 4.10-11). Yet from the beginning, there is an end in view: "The dust returns to the earth as it was, and the spirit returns to God who gave it" (Ecclesiastes 12.7).

Three Comparisons

God's relationship with time is different from ours. A millennium (1000 years) is hard for people to imagine, but God experiences time differently. Why? Because He is eternal, and we are mortal. Our vantage points are vastly different. For humans with brief lifespans, one thousand years seems long (it is equal to fifteen lifetimes). For God, it is like the passing of a single day or one night on guard duty for a soldier (an apt illustration of One who watches over all the earth). To convey how fast time passes from the human perspective, Moses gives three illustrations you can share with your child: floods, dreams, and grass.

> You sweep them away as with a flood; they are like a dream, like grass that is renewed in the morning: in the morning it flourishes and is renewed; in the evening it fades and withers. (Psalm 90:5-6)

Floods come swiftly and destructively, but the danger soon subsides and life goes on. So your life will go on and flourish after death. *Dreams* can be frightening, but you awake from them and return to your activities. You will awake to a better life after death. *Grass* that drinks in the morning dew can wilt under the hot afternoon sun, but more grass will grow tomorrow. You will revive and be refreshed on the morning of the resurrection. Passing years, decades, and centuries do not age or imperil God, but neither should they frighten the faithful.

Since God is the same yesterday, today, and forever (Hebrews 13.8), perishable people can benefit by looking to Him for wisdom. Relying on your own knowledge and power is laughable when your lifespan is so comparably small. Humans are weak and limited. God is almighty and infinite. His limitless wisdom and experience can be used to your advantage. His love is knowable, and His aid is accessible. Why not trust Him?

The suddenness of destructive storms is a reminder that time on earth is not only limited but uncertain. Only God knows how long a person will live. James warned Christians not to be overconfident about the amount of time left in their lives (James 4.13-15). Since life is impermanent and rapidly passing, use it well. You are as frail as a parched blade of grass and as fleeting as a morning mist. Therefore, do not take time for granted. It can be over in a flash, but that does not have to be scary. The end of earth time is not the end of all time.

Life Is Observed - *Read Psalm 90.7-11 with your child.*

When Moses connects death with God's anger, he may have been thinking of the wicked people who died in the flood or the disobedient Israelites who perished in the wilderness. However, it may also refer to God's displeasure with the negative effects of sin in the lives of His children. His anger is not like the uncontrollable outbursts of someone lacking self-restraint. Rather, it is an expression of His deep desire for people to have the best possible life. It bothers Him to see them suffering or settling for less than their best. He wants more for them.

When Moses says that God sets our iniquities before Him, it means that God is fully aware of every person's sins. Iniquities are thoughts, words, and actions characterized by unfairness to others. They are the product of a self-serving mindset. A lack of empathy causes people to place their feelings and desires above their neighbor's needs and well-being. Selfishness is immoral because it is hurtful.

God's Eyes (Psalm 90.8)

Even the "secret sins" that children hide from parents, teachers, or friends are fully known by God. What they do in the dark is exposed in the light of God's presence. Darkness can refer to nightfall, but it may also refer to spiritual darkness. Denial of wrongdoing and delusional justifications for sinful actions are forms of mental darkness. Excuses are lies told to oneself. Excuses do not deceive God. He knows every person's motives as well as their deeds. Hebrews 4.13 says, "And no creature is hidden from his sight, but all are naked and exposed to the eyes of him to whom we must give account."

God does not check in on people occasionally. He sees everything they do every single day. Moses explains, "All our days pass away under your wrath." "Wrath" does not mean God is grumpy and impossible to please. It means God hates sin with a passion because He desires a better life for His children. He is serious about sin and holds people accountable for selfish choices. They must face them to fix them. Through repentance, they correct what is harmful to themselves and hurtful to others. They put an end to things that damage their souls and relationships.

Human Sighs (Psalm 90.9)

As the days and years pass, people grow old and eventually die. Moses compares the growing weakness of the body to a sigh. A sigh is a long audible breath conveying sadness or fatigue. Loss of vitality is a sign of decline and the approaching end of life. The energy and exuberance of youth are replaced by groans due to aches and pains.

For many people, earth-time runs out sometime during their seventies or eighties. Dying later rather than sooner is not always a blessing. Toil (hard work) and trouble (perplexing problems) characterize all of life, but old age can be especially difficult due to increasing discomfort, disability, and dependency. Christians, however, view these difficulties as hints that something better is coming.

Time Flies (Psalm 90.10)

Regardless of how long one lives, it usually seems too short in the end. The years fly by, and the soul flies away. The longer one lives, the faster time seems to go. Flight is a beautiful image of the transition from earth-time to heaven-time. The soul departs the earth body in preparation for a better body. The new body will not age or die. It will not get sick or feel pain. It will not wear out. That is surely something to look forward to! In the meantime, how should time be utilized, especially given God's keen interest in your daily activities? Once again, Moses mentions God's anger and wrath to remind listeners that God knows everything they think, say, or do. Some people live without thought for God. Wise people seek His pleasure in all they do.

Life Is Spent - *Read Psalm 90.12-17 with your child.*

Wasted time cannot be retrieved. It is gone forever. Course corrections are possible, but you cannot reclaim what was misspent. To illustrate, think of investing money. Those who fail to invest while young will find it difficult to catch up when they are older. Starting at fifty is better than nothing, but not as good as starting at thirty. The principle of compounding interest works with time as well as money. Consequently, nowhere is self-control more needful than wise use of time. "In all *toil* there is profit, but mere *talk* tends only to poverty" (Proverbs 14.23). Success is a combination of information and application; wisdom and willpower; knowledge and action.

Teach Us to Number Our Days (Psalm 90.12)

Wisdom requires meditation as well as instruction. There is a profound difference between knowledge, understanding, and wisdom. Knowledge is wrapping your ears around an idea. Understanding is wrapping your head around it. Wisdom is wrapping your heart around God's word. Knowledge says, "time is valuable." Understanding says, "time is limited." Wisdom says, "invest it now."

Satisfy Us in the Morning with Your Steadfast Love (Psalm 90.14)

Moses asks God to pity the plight of His hapless children who cannot understand life without His aid (Psalm 90.13). "In the morning" means help is needed sooner rather than later. The sense of urgency is understandable given the misery that accompanies sin. When life is lived out of harmony with God's rules, the result is affliction. Evildoing brings pain and suffering, and life feels joyless rather than satisfying. In contrast, few things are more delightful than learning and living God's way (Psalm 90.15). God's "steadfast love" is evident in His willingness to reveal what people need to know. That is why one of the greatest proofs of God's love is the existence of the Bible. Moses mentions three ways God gladdens the hearts of eager learners.

#1 - Let Your Work Be Shown to Your Servants (Psalm 90.16)

When children observe God, they are awed by Him. By reading the Bible, they learn about God's work throughout human history (creation, redemption). Scripture shows them who God is through what He has done. They notice that God is always doing good (Genesis 1.4; Acts 10.38). They come to admire God's character and long to imitate His kindness and holiness.

#2 - Let the Favor of the Lord Be Upon Us (Psalm 90.17a)

When children obey God, they are blessed by Him. His favor rests upon those who heed His teachings. In describing the work of Paul and Barnabas at Iconium, Luke wrote, "So they remained for a long time, speaking boldly for the Lord, who bore witness to the word of his grace" (Acts 14.3). God is gracious to reveal Himself to mortals, and the changed lives of believers evidence His favor upon them. Like miracles, high morals are faith-confirming wonders.

#3 - Establish the work of our hands (Psalm 90.17b)

When children disobey God, they are disciplined by Him. They experience failure rather than favor. When applied effort produces worse results than doing nothing, God is sending a message. When words and actions backfire, His laws are being violated. Giving up is not the answer. To correct the situation, teach your children to stop doing what does not work and try a better way. Repentance and renewed effort are needed to turn things around. To "establish" means to set something up on a firm basis to ensure ongoing success. God-honoring goals backed up by biblical values are a foundation for future success. Plans that are not grounded in God's will are more likely to fail than to flourish (Matthew 7.26-27). Positive outcomes are the natural result of hearing and heeding God's word.

The Advantage

Children who do not grasp the meaning of time are severely disadvantaged. If they do not grasp the brevity of time, it slips away. If they do not sense the value of time, it cannot be redeemed. If they do not seize the opportunity of time, it causes regret. Your job is to help your child comprehend the significance and utility of time so they can use it for good ends. Understanding time gives your children a distinct advantage in life. They can choose spiritual progress over worldly pleasure. They can delight God rather than debase themselves. They can invest their time rather than squander it.

Practicing the Psalms

To be successful, number your days.

Text Questions:

1. What is set before the light of God's presence?
2. How do you get a heart of wisdom?
3. What are a thousand years like to God?
4. How many are the years of our lives?
5. Name two things that fill human years.

Discussion Questions:

1. Why do people waste time? What are the dangers?
2. What are the benefits of using time well?
3. How is God like a dwelling place?
4. How is death like a flood? Like a dream? Like grass?
5. Why was the Prodigal sad? What made him glad?

Parent/Child Exercise: Sit down with your child and make a list of ten time wasters. Follow up by making a list of ten time winners. Over the next week, do each item on the last list together. Discuss the difference between "finding" time and "making" time to do good.

Chapter Eleven

Psalm 119 - Learn Your ABCs

Wesley Walker

How can a young man keep his way pure? By guarding it according to your word. With my whole heart I seek you; let me not wander from your commandments! I have stored up your word in my heart, that I might not sin against you. Blessed are you, O LORD; teach me your statutes! With my lips I declare all the rules of your mouth. In the way of your testimonies I delight as much as in all riches. I will meditate on your precepts and fix my eyes on your ways. I will delight in your statutes; I will not forget your word. (Psalm 119.9-16)

I have three young children. We have spent the better part of a decade teaching ABCs, phonics, and the basics of reading to them. The ABCs are the first and most foundational step to learning. Without the ABCs, you cannot master the rest of your academic career. It is no surprise, then, that when the psalmist wants to relate the basics of spiritual wisdom, he does so using an acrostic of the Hebrew alphabet. Just like our kids and grandkids begin their learning by mastering the ABCs, we begin the journey of wisdom by learning the ABCs of faith.

The most rudimentary teaching of the Bible is that the foundational wisdom of life is found in the word of God. We teach our kids "the B.I.B.L.E., yes that is the book for me" because we understand that a life built on the word of God is the wisest and best of all lives. Wisdom is the ability to see the natural outcomes of your decisions and to choose the best path. For followers of Jesus, the best path is the one that leads to a life of faithfulness to God.

Helping our kids choose the right path in life lies at the heart of many parental decisions. We want them to choose the best path, and we know that the best path for them is the path of wisdom. It will give them a foundation for success in all areas of their life. Yet the choice is theirs and not ours. So how do we help our kids see the word of God as the source of this wisdom? Psalm 119 was written to answer this very question. Teach your children these six traits of God's word:

#1 - It Is Trustworthy (Psalm 119.160)

The first reason God's word should be treasured is that it is dependable. It alone provides you with unqualified truth. Verse 160 says the "totality of your word is truth." That means each part of God's word is truth. Each command, statute, and teaching is completely reliable. Sometimes people question if there is such a thing as absolute truth in this world. The psalmist makes it clear that truth does exist, and that it is found in the word of God. The Bible is the ultimate source of wisdom because each teaching of God contains truth that improves your quality of life. Directly or in principle, the word of God has valuable lessons on every relevant issue your children will face during their lifetimes (2 Peter 1.3):

- How to be good friends
- How to live well with parents
- How to do well in school
- How to be successful at work
- How to please God

God's word has stood the test of time because it has met every need, withstood every challenge, and proved itself trustworthy time after time.

#2 - It Guides You (Psalm 119.105)

A second reason God's word should be cherished is that it is a lamp that guides our path. One year, for my oldest child's birthday, we did a camp theme party. We had a fishing game, grilled hotdogs, and hamburgers, and watched a Mickey Mouse camping special. As part of that night's festivities, we turned off all the lights in one of the rooms and gave each kid a flashlight. With the flashlight, they were supposed to follow a map we had hidden on the wall. They could only see the map by using their flashlights, and whoever found the path would win. The word of God is a spiritual lamp for our children. In a world that obscures the way of God, the word illuminates the right path for us. It shows us the way to live a life that pleases God—a life of wisdom. The psalmist says, "your word is a lamp to my feet and a light to my path."

#3 - It Protects You (Psalm 119.9)

A third reason God's word should be appreciated is that it keeps us from living a worthless life. We only have one life. There is a popular saying from a few years ago that put this succinctly: "YOLO." It stands for "You Only Live Once." It is a reminder that since we only have one life, we should make the most of it. Teaching kids how to live the most worthwhile life is the goal of every godly parent and grandparent. We want to help our kids make the most of life. "Making the most of life" has a different definition for Jesus' followers than for the world. The world's version of making the most of life could be pursuing every pleasure in reckless living. However, for disciples of Jesus, making the most of life is living a life that honors God. The word of God gives us the guidance we need to lead a meaningful life. It keeps us away from sin and puts us on a path to the most fulfilling and consequential life possible.

#4 - It Saves You (Psalm 119.41)

A fourth reason God's word should be adored is that it shows us the path to salvation (Psalm 119.81). Despite our best efforts, we all need saving. Psalm 119 celebrates God's redemption, mercy, and salvation. This salvation is unavailable to the wicked and faithless. It is only available to those who keep the law of God and follow His statutes. Those who show their love for God in obedience have a special relationship with Him. This is the relationship we want our children and grandchildren to have with God. It is a connection based on the covenant made possible by Christ's death on the cross. Extending the covenant proves that God wants a relationship with us. Entering the covenant shows that we want a relationship with Him. Our eagerness to keep the covenant declares that He is our God, and we are His people (Psalm 119.166-168). As His people, we long to keep His commandments and share in His faithful love (Psalm 90.174-175).

#5 - It Blesses You (Psalm 119.2)

A fifth reason God's word is beloved is that it gives us a life of blessings. The psalmist reminds us, "Blessed are those whose way is blameless, who walk in the Law of the LORD. Blessed are those who keep His testimonies and seek Him with all their heart." The thesis of the psalm is that the person who obeys the Law of God is blessed by Him. A blessed life is a God-approved life. Wisdom literature explains how to live a God-approved life. When their days on earth are over, we want our children to hear the words "well done." By following the decrees, statutes, and commands of God, they will live a God-approved life.

#6 - It Delights You (Psalm 119.14)

A sixth reason God's word should be prized is that it delights you (Psalm 119.24,77,174). The ABCs of Psalm 119 are not merely about the practical benefits of God's word. They are also about the deep desire we should have for hearing our Father's voice. We do not want our children to robotically follow God's commands (1 John 5.3). Rather, we want them to have a heart that thirsts to know God like a deer pants for water (Psalm 42.1).

My kids delight in different things. They have sports they love to play, shows they love to watch, and crafts they love to create. My youngest just finished his first baseball season, and he delighted in each practice and game. My middle child could sit for hours painting or drawing because she delights in it. My oldest loves being around her friends because it brings her much joy. I hope they also find delight in the word of God. The benefits of delighting in God's word will far outweigh the benefits of other activities.

As parents or grandparents, our goal should be to help our kids delight in God's law. We do this by modeling that delight by reading our Bibles in front of them, by showing the enjoyment we get from learning new truths about God, and by living a life that puts those words into action. Children do not merely need to hear how important the word of God is; they need to see that we believe what we say.

Seek a God-Approved Life

Growing in wisdom is a lifelong pursuit. From their earliest days, encourage your children to live the best possible life they can, making the most of every moment. The best possible life is not merely a life of success by the standards of our world (health, wealth, status). The best life is a God-approved life. It comes from delighting in and obeying God's word, the source of all wisdom. The Bible reveals truth that guides, saves, and blesses us. It is the ultimate map for living a meaningful life. Teaching children God's word gives them far greater benefits than learning their ABCs.

Oh how I love your law! It is my meditation all the day. Your commandment makes me wiser than my enemies, for it is ever with me. I have more understanding than all my teachers, for your testimonies are my meditation. I understand more than the aged, for I keep your precepts. I hold back my feet from every evil way, in order to keep your word. I do not turn aside from your rules, for you have taught me. How sweet are your words to my taste, sweeter than honey to my mouth! Through your precepts I get understanding; therefore I hate every false way. (Psalm 119.97-104)

Practicing the Psalms

To be successful, know your ABCs.

Text Questions:
1. Who is blessed according to the start of Psalm 119?
2. What are some often repeated words in the Psalm?
3. What does Psalm 119.160 mean to you?
4. Help your kids memorize Psalm 119.105
5. How many verses are there in Psalm 119?

Discussion Questions:
1. Share a time when you gained wisdom from God's word.
2. Which of the six benefits of God's word is your favorite?
3. What is your favorite section of Scripture?
4. When has God's word provided you with comfort?
5. How do you show your delight in God's word?

Parent/Child Exercise:
Choose a section of the Bible to read together with your child/grandchild and talk about how it guides your life and delights your soul.

Chapter Twelve

Psalm 121 - Lift Up Your Eyes

Doug Burleson

I lift up my eyes to the hills. From where does my help come? My help comes from the LORD, who made heaven and earth. He will not let your foot be moved; he who keeps you will not slumber. Behold, he who keeps Israel will neither slumber nor sleep. The LORD is your keeper; the LORD is your shade on your right hand. The sun shall not strike you by day, nor the moon by night. The LORD will keep you from all evil; he will keep your life. The LORD will keep your going out and your coming in from this time forth and forevermore. (Psalm 121.1-8)

Every parent can remember the moment when their children took their first steps. Those steps were likely awkward, and for the parent, scary. It required all of their strength to resist grabbing up the wobbly child to keep them from falling. Despite the clumsiness and anxiousness, they walked! In our case, we celebrated that big moment and then realized that their mobility changed everything. As much as parents want to help their children, there are moments when our power to intervene and provide what is needed falls short.

In Psalm 121, God is the single source of help named. The keyword used to describe God means "keep" or "keeper" and occurs six times in eight verses. As ancient Israelites traveled to Jerusalem to observe their holy days, God's people would sing this psalm and other "Psalms of Ascent" (Psalms 120-134) as a means of praising God and petitioning His protection.

Abraham, Isaac, Jacob, and Esau are called sojourners in the book of Genesis. God's people have always been on the move and will be on the move until Christ returns. Being on the move means that we need help along the way. Though the scenery and centuries change, every disciple is on a journey. Our success depends on trusting in the One who has promised to help us on our way.

A Help Greater than the Hills

Families that travel over hills today seldom think about the challenges ancient Israelites faced when traveling over mountains. While modern travelers might be concerned about getting their brakes checked or making sure there is enough gas in the tank, in antiquity, mountains provided special challenges. They were difficult to cross and provided thieves opportunities to prey on the tired and vulnerable.

The writer of Psalm 121 has travel in mind. The very first verse asks an important question, "From where does my help come?" Amid this second Psalm of Ascents, he notes that God will not allow our foot to slip (3), and He will guard our going out and coming in (8).

If God is our Keeper, why lift our eyes to the hills? Maybe the hills provided a place where one could hide. Perhaps the high places signified closer access to God or a sense of His nearness. Another answer is more likely. The psalmist is reminding us that we should trust in the One who made the hills and everything else in heaven and on earth (Psalm 121.2). Psalm 123.1 exclaims, "To you I lift up my eyes, to you who are enthroned in the heavens!" Psalm 124.8 notes, "Our help is in the name of the Lord, who made heaven and earth." God, the Keeper, wants to help us on our journey. This raises three questions as we travel through life:

• Who will help me when I fall?

• Who will help me when I get tired?

• Who will help me when I might get burned?

Parents, it is not your job to protect your children from every bump on the road. Rather, it is to help them learn and grow from each experience as they faithfully continue the journey. You must point them to the One who will sustain them along the way.

A Keeper that Will Not Let You Fall

The first time I took my family to the Grand Canyon I was a nervous wreck. After flipping through a book in the gift shop that detailed the many ways that people died at the Grand Canyon, we took our young children to see the 6,001-foot-deep ravine. The Grand Canyon was majestic to behold, and we had a great visit there, but my primary concern was keeping my kids back from the edge. We took some pictures and enjoyed the beautiful scenes, but I was still uneasy.

After my experience of keeping my kids back from the edge of the canyon, I have a greater appreciation for God who has promised that He will not allow a traveler's foot to slip (Psalm 121.3; Psalm 66.9). Does this mean that we will never stumble? No, but in faith, we will rebound from every fall and press on. God will protect His people from "all evil" and keep their souls (Psalm 121.7). While this help is available to all people everywhere, only those with knowledge and discretion will be surefooted. Proverbs 3.23 speaks of knowledge and discretion helping sojourners to, "walk on your way securely and your foot will not stumble." The new mother, Hannah, knew this truth well. After the birth of Samuel, she exclaimed of God, "He will guard the feet of his faithul ones" (1 Samuel 2.9). Falls are inevitable in life, but we can get back up through faith in the God who keeps us.

A Keeper That Does Not Sleep

Even parents with the best intentions get sleepy. On long trips, you can spend a lot of time in the driver's seat and consume lots of caffeine to stay alert. But fatigue is not limited to those in the driver's seat. Have you ever taken care of a sick loved one? Keeping watch through the night can be difficult due to sleep deprivation. Sometimes we sleep through alarms or doze off when we ought to be alert, so what will assure travelers that they will be safe when they get tired?

Twice, the psalmist reminds readers that God does not sleep: "He will not let your foot be moved; he who keeps you will not slumber. Behold, he who keeps Israel will neither slumber nor sleep" (Psalm 121.3-4). Sometimes people doubt this because of what David called God's eyelid test: "his eyelids test the children of man" (Psalm 11.4). Like the grandparent who seems to know what you're up to even when her eyes are closed, God sees what is happening though some doubt if He can.

God is always awake to take it all in. Recently, a friend told me about a time of testing when he stayed up all night praying. He finally realized that there was no reason for him to stay awake since God was already going to be up anyway. The Bible says, "unless the Lord watches over the city, the watchman stays awake in vain" (Proverbs 127.1b).

130

Human guards get tired, and drivers get distracted, but God never fails.

When reading your Bible, have you ever noticed how many bad things happened when people slept? Samson's sleep allowed Delilah to cut his hair (Judges 16.14-19). Saul's sleep made him vulnerable to David (1 Samuel 26.7-12). Not even those in the Garden of Gethsemane could stay awake long enough to keep watch (Matthew 26.40-45). Falling asleep while perched in a window cost Eutychus his life (Acts 20.9). Does this mean we should not sleep? Of course not. However, it does remind us of our need for protection when we are vulnerable, which includes when we sleep. Take comfort in the fact that God will be up even when we sleep.

A Keeper That Shades

For modern motorists, a sun visor can hide the sun's glare, and air conditioning can bring relief from the sun's heat. For ancient Israelites who meandered through the Judean hills on the way to Jerusalem, the sun was a serious threat. What relief could be found for those who were in danger of succumbing to heat stroke? Psalm 121.5 declares, "the Lord is your shade at your right hand."

Is this a literal shade like the kind God provided Jonah as he looked out over Nineveh after he finished preaching (Jonah 4.6)? While God can be praised for literal shade, He can also be praised for providing spiritual rest and relief. On your faith journey, there is no greater place to find refuge than in the "shadow of the Almighty" (Psalm 91.1).

A Help that Lasts Forever

As you journey, how long can the stability, sober-mindedness, and shelter of God last? God's help lasts "from this time forth and forevermore" (Psalm 121.8). Even the best warranties on earth only last a few years. They are here today and gone tomorrow. The help God offers is eternal.

In Psalm 121 we learn that God is our Help (1-2), our Maker (2), our Keeper (5, 7), our Shade (5), our Protector (7), and our eternally vigilant Guard (8). As you journey through life, there is no better direction to look in than God's direction. As you travel, do not be discouraged when trials come. Some doubt that God will guard their comings and goings since bad things sometimes happen to good people. Trust that God is near even in hard times.

As Christians journey through life, they will experience trials. Psalm 121 does not promise that God's help will meet your preferences. It does promise that He will be there for you and keep you. The devil does not want you to reach your heavenly destination, but God has promised to protect the faithful on the road to glory. As you and your child journey through life, God's loving presence is certain though His methods are not always predictable.

What life lessons can you teach your children using Psalm 121? Teach them to be willing and eager to ask for God's help. When times are tough, encourage them to press on in faith knowing God will give them sure footing. Remind them to rest well because God is always awake. Promise them that on the most severe days, God will provide protective shade. Assure them that God is their Helper and Keeper— always.

Practicing the Psalms

To be successful, look to the hills.

Text Questions:
1. Why were hills a secure place?
2. How is the keyword usually translated in Psalm 121?
3. How is God described in Psalm 121?
4. What does God protect His people from?
5. How long does God's protection last?

Discussion Questions:
1. Share a time in your life when you were really scared.
2. How will God help us as we journey through life?
3. When has God's protection been evident in your life?
4. Will bad things never happen to us?
5. How would you describe God's protection for us?

Parent/Child Exercise: Next time you go on a family trip take time to read Psalm 121 before you leave. Gather the family around, read the psalm, and then pray to God using some of the language from Psalm 121. Pray that He does not allow your feet to slip on your way. Pray that He will continue to keep you from all harm. Pray that He watches over your comings and goings not only as you travel to and from your destination, but also as you journey faithfully throughout life.

Chapter 13

Psalm 139 - Run Toward God

Andrew Phillips

I have never been good with directions. I can follow a map, and I can take instructions from a navigation app, but if I am left on my own, it won't be long before I am lost. Years ago, I was part of a group returning from a mission trip in Europe. On our last day of the trip, my friend and I were standing in a long line for a museum in a densely packed downtown area. I decided to venture down the winding road to a shop I could see in the distance while my friend held my place in line.

The shop was further away than I thought, and I checked out another store while I was there. By the time I finished, I was completely disoriented and took the wrong road to get back to my friend. It dawned on me that I didn't speak the local language and didn't know where I was going. I can still remember the rising panic.

Have you ever been lost? It can be a miserable feeling. As difficult as my experience was, I also remember the relief I felt when I finally turned a corner and saw my friend from a distance. We feel safe when we know we are not alone. Psalm 139 reminds us that even when we feel alone, we are not really by ourselves. It is a powerful reminder that we are not stranded, and we can feel safe knowing that God is with us. Use this Psalm to teach your children three encouraging truths that will grant them peace amid life's difficulties and uncertainties.

Truth #1: God knows where you are all the time.

> Where shall I go from your Spirit? Or where shall I flee from your presence? If I ascend to heaven, you are there! If I make my bed in Sheol, you are there. If I take the wings of the morning and dwell in the uttermost parts of the sea, even there your hand shall lead me, and your right hand shall hold me. If I say, "Surely the darkness shall cover me, and the light about me be night," even the darkness is not dark to you; the night is bright as the day, for darkness is as light with you. (Psalm 139.7-12)

The psalm begins by praising God's knowledge of us. "O Lord, You have searched me and known me. You know when I sit down and when I rise up. You understand my thought from afar" (Psalm 139.1-2). Have you ever tried to explain something to someone and found it difficult to put your thoughts into words? Even when you are doing your best to communicate, you can see the confusion in the other person's eyes. You never have to worry about that with God. He always knows exactly what is weighing on our minds and hearts.

God not only understands you, but He also sees you. There is nowhere you can go outside of His presence (Psalm 139.7-12). As Jonah found out when he boarded a ship to Tarshish, you can't run from God. The psalmist depicts the futility of trying to find a spot where you can hide from God. It would be like a child playing hide-and-go-seek who covers his eyes and convinces himself no one can see him. His lack of sight has no bearing on others.

In the same way, your imaginings of a good hiding spot have no bearing on God's ability to see all. The highest heavens, the depths of the unseen realm, and the remotest part of the seas are not beyond God's view. He knows where you are and where you've been. He sees your actions, but He also knows your intentions. "And no creature is hidden from his sight, but all are naked and exposed to the eyes of him to whom we must give account" (Hebrews 4.13). God knows you inside out.

Knowing that God sees all can be comforting or frightening. If you do things you shouldn't do or dwell on thoughts you shouldn't think, it can make you nervous to know those things aren't secret from God. But when you seek to live for God and honor Him in every aspect of your life, knowing He sees all gives you strength. No matter what you face, God is with you.

Truth #2: God knows how you were made.

> For you formed my inward parts; you knitted me together in my mother's womb. I praise you, for I am fearfully and wonderfully made. Wonderful are your works; my soul knows it very well. My frame was not hidden from you, when I was being made in secret, intricately woven in the depths of the earth. Your eyes saw my unformed substance; in your book were written, every one of them, the days that were formed for me, when as yet there was none of them. (Psalm 139.13-16)

Advancements in technology enable parents to know a lot about children before they are born. From sonograms to 3D images, we now get detailed pictures of a growing child in the womb. But Psalm 139.13-16 gives us an even more vivid description of a child before birth:

When I look in the mirror, there are things I wish I could change. I've started noticing gray hair in recent years, and I've always wished my feet were smaller. Chances are, you also notice those kinds of things when looking in the mirror. But this psalm reminds us that every single person has been specially made by God. Regardless of your perception, God sees a lovingly made human being.

This is also true when it comes to your abilities. Have you ever wished you excelled in a specific area? Sometimes, we look at a talented person and lose sight of how God has uniquely equipped us. In the early church, Christians were given miraculous gifts to confirm God's message. Paul told the church at Corinth that the Holy Spirit distributed those gifts to each person just as He wills. When it came to those miraculous gifts, they had what God had given them. When it comes to our talents and abilities today, we have what God has given us. Psalm 139 reminds us that God has a plan for how we use our gifts in His service.

Truth #3: God knows what you are feeling.

> Oh that you would slay the wicked, O God! O men of blood, depart from me! They speak against you with malicious intent; your enemies take your name in vain. Do I not hate those who hate you, O LORD? And do I not loathe those who rise up against you? I hate them with complete hatred; I count them my enemies. Search me, O God, and know my heart! Try me and know my thoughts! And see if there be any grievous way in me, and lead me in the way everlasting! (Psalm 139.19-24)

Verses 19 and 22 are surprising to read. The psalmist expresses anger toward enemies and asks God to take vengeance. What do we do when we read something like that? There are several Psalms where we find language like this, as the psalmist vents deep emotions which are often unpleasant.

Even these passages can encourage us, though. First, instead of taking action, the psalmist is leaving vengeance up to God. This is a biblical principle we need to remember. Paul wrote, "If possible, so far as it depends on you, live peaceably with all. Beloved, never avenge yourselves, but leave it to the wrath of God, for it is written, 'Vengeance is mine, I will repay, says the Lord'" (Romans 12.18-19).

When people make us angry, we need to resist the urge to take action and get revenge on our own. Movies and TV shows often glorify "vigilante justice" where one person acts as judge and jury to get revenge on lawbreakers. God reminds us that He is the ultimate judge and that our actions should honor His justice. Rather than harming others, Paul advised a more compassionate course: "If your enemy is hungry, feed him; if he is thirsty, give him something to drink; for by so doing you will heap burning coals on his head. Do not be overcome by evil, but overcome evil with good" (Romans 12.20-21).

Though he exercises self-restraint, the psalmist is comfortable expressing his feelings to God. Sometimes we are embarrassed by our emotions. We may even feel guilty saying out loud how we feel. But God made us and knows us. He understands how we are feeling, and He desires that we be honest with Him.

In the Old Testament, a faithful servant of God named Job deals with the terrible loss of his children, wealth, and health. His wife tells him to curse God, while his friends tell him he must have sinned and ought to repent. In this book, Job reveals his deepest emotions and has some harsh things to say. Despite his confusion and frustration, we read a surprising line at the end of the book. God commends Job and calls on him to pray for his friends who wrongly accused him.

> Now therefore take seven bulls and seven rams and go to my servant Job and offer up a burnt offering for yourselves. And my servant Job shall pray for you, for I will accept his prayer not to deal with you according to your folly. For you have not spoken of me what is right, as my servant Job has. (Job 42.8)

Job's difficult emotions did not disqualify him from being faithful, and neither will yours. You just need to bring them to God with honesty and transparency.

The psalm ends with an important plea: "Search me, O God, and know my heart! Try me and know my thoughts! And see if there be any grievous way in me, and lead me in the way everlasting!" (Psalm 139.23-24). The psalmist asks God to uncover any anxious or hurtful thoughts he needs to address. This provides you with a healthy pattern to follow: once you share your emotions with God, ask Him to help you identify unhealthy thoughts so you can follow His will instead of your own.

Run to God

When your children feel lonely or fearful, remind them that God is always near. Have them name the farthest or funniest places they can think of, and then guarantee them that God is there. When your children feel insecure, assure them that God loves them and will never stop loving them. God is not pleased when they sin, but He never stops loving them because they sin.

God is good because His love is trustworthy. He always wants the best for you. He wants you to learn from your mistakes rather than repeat them. He wants you to be sorry and do better. When you do wrong, God hurts for you and will hold you responsible, but that is because He loves you —not because He has stopped loving you. He wants you to draw closer to Him rather than run away. Run to His arms. He is always waiting.

Practicing the Psalms

To feel more successful, run toward God.

Text Questions:
1. When does God know the words we are going to say?
2. Where can you hide from God's presence?
3. Who was the prophet who tried to run from God?
4. Name a reason you should give thanks to God.
5. Who stayed faithful after losing his possessions, family, and health?

Discussion Questions:
1. How does it make you feel to know God is always with you?
2. Are there times when that fact might make us uncomfortable?
3. Why is it valuable to know that God created each of us for a purpose?
4. What do the scriptures tell us about the way we should treat our enemies?
5. Why is it hard to express harsh or embarrassing emotions to God in prayer?
6. How could praying about them help us manage those difficult feelings?

Parent/Child Exercise: Get out some of your children's first baby pictures (you may also have images of them in the womb). If you have a video of them as a child, let them watch their younger selves. Tell them how it felt to see each of them for the first time, to watch their tiny hands and feet and lock eyes with them. Share the emotions you remember experiencing at that moment.

Next, get out some of your baby pictures. If they have never seen them before, those pictures will probably make them laugh. As you look at these images, reflect on the fact that you were once a baby, fearfully and wonderfully made.

Then, go through pictures of people you know. Maybe you can use a school yearbook or scroll through some pictures on your phone. As you look at each person, ask if they can imagine that individual as a baby. How does it change our perspective when we realize that everyone is fearfully and wonderfully made?

Afterword - Build Wisely

Aubrey Johnson

Unless the LORD builds the house, those who build it labor in vain. Unless the LORD watches over the city, the watchman stays awake in vain. It is in vain that you rise up early and go late to rest, eating the bread of anxious toil; for he gives to his beloved sleep. Behold, children are a heritage from the LORD, the fruit of the womb a reward. Like arrows in the hand of a warrior are the children of one's youth. Blessed is the man who fills his quiver with them! He shall not be put to shame when he speaks with his enemies in the gate. (Psalm 127.1-5)

Psalm 127 is a fitting conclusion to a book on parenting by the Psalms. Tradition says that David dedicated this psalm to his son, Solomon, the builder of the first Temple. Just as the faith of David and Solomon led to the successful completion of God's house of worship, faith is crucial for building up godly households today. Faith is the difference between success and failure.

Parents who trust in God's guidance and providence are less apprehensive and exhausted than those who depend on their own wisdom. Christian mothers and fathers enjoy the peace that comes from partnering with God. My prayer is that this book will help you ground your children in biblical faith and values. Rest assured, your labors will not be in vain if you parent by the Psalms.

God's Spirit watches over those who fill their hearts with His holy word. Instead of being anxious, diligently teach your children the mind-expanding, soul-enlarging, life-enhancing truths contained in the Psalms. May the architect of eternity build up your family in the most holy faith, and may He give you the sweet sleep of a conscience that trusts in His infinite power and love.

Practicing the Psalms

To be faithful and successful…

1. Choose good friends.
   Psalm 1
2. Shine like stars.
   Psalm 19
3. Think healthy thoughts.
   Psalm 23
4. Be correctable.
   Psalm 25
5. Unlock your power.
   Psalm 27
6. Live joyfully.
   Psalm 32
7. Ignore the noise.
   Psalm 37
8. Count your blessings.
   Psalm 46
9. Use your scars.
   Psalm 51
10. Number your days.
    Psalm 90
11. Know your ABCs.
    Psalm 119
12. Look to the hills.
    Psalm 121
13. Run toward God.
    Psalm 139

A Parent's Primer in the Psalms

1. There are 150 psalms.

2. Psalms is the longest book in the Bible.

3. Psalm 119 is the longest psalm and the longest chapter in the Bible.

4. Psalm 117 is the shortest psalm and the shortest chapter in the Bible.

5. The Book of Psalms is an anthology (published collection of poems).

6. The Book of Psalms is divided into five sections:

   - Book 1 (Psalms 1-41).
   - Book 2 (Psalms 42-72).
   - Book 3 (Psalms 73-89).
   - Book 4 (Psalms 90-106).
   - Book 5 (Psalms 107-150).

7. Each section closes with a doxology or benediction.

8. Writers include David, Asaph, Solomon, Moses, Ethan the Ezrahite, Heman the Ezrahite, and the sons of Korah.

9. Superscriptions may indicate the writer, occasion, or musical direction for leaders.

10. Verse numbers were first printed in 1509.

11. Primary types of psalms include the following:
    1. Hymns (praising God's work in history).
    2. Communal Laments (expressing collective sorrow).
    3. Individual Laments (expressing personal sorrow).
    4. Royal Psalms (involving the king or God as King).
    5. Individual Thanksgiving Psalms (expressing gratitude for deliverance).
    6. Pilgrimage Psalms (sung while traveling to Jerusalem).
12. Most psalms are individual laments.
13. Parallelism (symmetry of thought) is the leading feature of this genre of literature.
    1. Synonymous parallelism (one line restates the idea of another).
    2. Antithetic parallelism (one line expresses the opposite of another).
    3. Expansive parallelism (one line amplifies the idea of another).
14. Psalms were written for praise, prayer, and practical instruction.

More Books by Aubrey Johnson

My Father's House

Parenting by the Parables

Parenting by the Psalms

The Best Husband Ever

The Barnabas Factor

Renewing Your Spiritual Life

Music Matters

Spiritual Patriots

Love More, Sin Less

The Seed Principle

God's Game Plan

Consider One Another

Bold Faith

Dynamic Deacons

Dynamic Deacons Companion Workbook

The Deacon's Wife

Successful Shepherds

Effective Elders

Organized Overseers

Meeting Well Workbook

Get Fit! Church Growth through Church Health

Parenting by the Parables

A Guide to Spiritual Parenting

Aubrey Johnson, Editor

Made in the USA
Columbia, SC
20 March 2023

13899255R00085